Healing with Shamanism

Healing with
SHAMANISM

Practices and Traditions to Restore and Balance the Self

Jaime Meyer, MA

**ROCKRIDGE
PRESS**

Interior and Cover Designer: Julie Schrader
Art Producer: Hannah Dickerson
Editor: Jesse Aylen
Production Editor: Rachel Taenzler

Photography credits: iStock/Benjavisa, cover and p. 97; iStock/ivanastar, back cover and pp. XI, 9-27, 38-39, 46-50, 58-69, 91-92, 107-114, 123-124, 133-134; Alamy Stock Photo/Sabena Jane Blackbird, pp. II, VIII, 71, 115; iStock/flovie, pp. VI, VII, XII, 1, 32, 33, 72, 73, 98, 99, 126, 127; iStock/nubumbim, pp. 10, 12, 13, 15, 17, 21, 26; Shutterstock/Trikona, p. 35; Shutterstock/Forager, p. 44; iStock/ tigerstrawberry, p. 46; Shutterstock/Foxyliam, pp. 47, 48 (top), 107, 110, 112-114; Shutterstock/lamnee, p. 48 (bottom); iStock/feirin, p. 49; Shutterstock/Mila-nana, p. 50; Shutterstock/Peratek, p. 58; Shutterstock/olly, p. 59; Shutterstock/ DianaFinch, pp. 60, 62, 64, 66, 69; Shutterstock/Reinke Fox, p. 61; Shutterstock/ Vector Tradition, p. 63; Shutterstock/ViSnezh, p. 65 (top); iStock/animatedfunk, p. 65 (bottom); Shutterstock/Maria Sem, p. 67; Shutterstock/Big Boy, p. 68; iStock/DubrovskayaD, p. 75; Shutterstock/J. Palys, p. 81; Shutterstock/Coldmoon Photoproject, p. 82; Shutterstock/Cagla Acikgoz, p. 83; Shutterstock/Sebastian Janicki, p. 84; Shutterstock/Sergey Lavrentev, p. 85; Shutterstock/movit, p. 86; Shutterstock/Tamara Kulikova, p. 87; Shutterstock/Zelenskaya, p. 88; Shutter-stock/bjphotographs, pp. 89, 90; Shutterstock/Channarong Pherngjanda, pp. 108, 111; Shutterstock/Suwi19, p. 109; iStock/Ko_Te, p. 131.

ISBN: Print 978-1-64611-855-7 | eBook 978-1-64611-856-4
R0

I dedicate this book to my teachers, and their teachers, and their teachers, and to the beautiful Mother Earth. May my words, thoughts, and actions be good in the sight of each and every one of you.

─────────────────────────────

Contents

Introduction

Right now, you are being supported by the land beneath and around you. The land is holding and caring for you; from the waters and winds to fields and hills and the light and warmth of the sun, you're living inside a great conspiracy of caring. You're nestled inside a web of life that wraps itself around and through you, connecting you to every other strand and junction. You're not only connected outward but also inward, for the land is also inside you: in the earth, air, fire, and water that make up your body. You are a small bit of Mother Earth's body, as is everything else on this planet. You are animal skin with ocean poured in, and with the light and breath of infinity poured in. You're not only connected outward and inward but also upward, for the stars and galaxies, too, are made of the same land. You are connected backward though time to all the ones who have moved across the land before you, and to all those coming soon—or not so soon—into this earthly realm. The land is filled with power to heal, to give and restore life, as well as to bring passion, meaning, and purpose. As you'll learn in the pages that follow, shamanic practices call on these powers in humility, with love, gratitude, and respect.

I've been studying the shamanic path since 1983. In my life, I've studied many religions and spiritual practices, including earning a master's degree from a seminary in my home state of Minnesota. I've studied with a variety of shamanic teachers from various traditions. My seminary professors, following the ancient Greeks, taught me that "an unexamined life is not worth living." My shamanic teachers, each in their own way, taught me that "an unlived live is not worth examining."

Shamanism as a spiritual practice is a path of power. If that phrase sounds daunting to you, that's good. The web of life is infused with great power beyond human comprehension, and shamanic practice is all about asking those powers to work with you, and to teach, guide, refine, and open you to greater life power. In this book, we will embark upon a learning and healing journey that I hope will fill you with wonder, love, and the power to help you live in restorative wholeness.

Together we'll see just how global and broadly historical the fundamental ideas and practices are, and how they're shared by people as disparate as those of the rolling North American prairie, steamy South American rain forest, windswept Scottish highlands, monsoon-soaked mountains of Southeast Asia, and ice-covered subarctic tundra.

You'll learn about working respectfully and safely with the spirits of nature and guides from the spirit world. You'll learn how to add to your own shamanic-inspired toolbox that includes the drum and rattle, the singing voice, the dancing body, the nuanced skill of prayer and intention, and the all-important sacred imagination upon whose wings we dream, meditate, and ride to the spirit world.

You'll come away from this book with an organic understanding of shamanic healing practices and a set of practices to foster your own healing and help build a life more powerfully aligned with Spirit.

That said, know that I don't see shamanic healing as a complete replacement for Western allopathic medicine or therapy. The earth has given us many ways of healing ourselves and others, and all should be considered on our great journey.

Chapter 1

The Origins and Spread of Shamanism

In this chapter, we will explore the birth of what many call humanity's first spiritual practice. We will delve into the origins of shamanism, offer important definitions of its healing practices, and introduce you to some of its most common healing tools.

Shamanism Defined

Somewhere in the shadows of time, human beings became aware that they were part of a larger cosmos. We began to realize we are swimming in powers greater than us, powers that determine our life and death, health or illness, abundance or scarcity. The Spirit of Creation decided the time was right to make humans sentient. We experienced the first glimmer of the immense game played between chaos and order, and the understanding of the transcendent union of body, mind, and spirit. We began to ask how we can better know these Great Powers and work within them—or even influence them. The sacred imagination was born inside us, and shamanism, humanity's first spiritual practice, began to take form.

For tens of thousands of years, shamanic practice has been evolving, but it always asks the same fundamental question: Given what I know now, how can I better understand, work with, and affect the Great Powers of life, death, chaos, and order? Shamanism is not a classically defined religion, since there are no official sacred scriptures, dogmas, or priestly hierarchies. Instead, shamanism has always been a localized, healing-centered practice individualized by each person within their unique cultural context and surroundings.

Every tribe of people has had their own name for the role that we now call the *shaman*. That particular name originates from the Tungusic word *šaman* and is commonly said to mean "the one who sees." *Šaman* can also be translated as "one who is excited, heated, moved, or raised," pointing to the ecstatic practices many shamans perform. The word was popularized by European anthropologists in the 1800s and soon became the Western world's generic term for indigenous healers, even though that word is not used by any of the other groups of people living near the Evenki. Indeed, each has their own specific word.

Even with thousands of different global influences, shamanic healing has, throughout time and culture, involved some common practices and tools. Trance-inducing rhythm using drums, rattles, gongs, or other instruments are common, as is singing, dancing, prayer, meditations, fasting, hallucinogens, time spent alone in nature, and visualizations that bring people into contact with otherworldly helpers that can offer healing guidance. All of these cross-cultural practices open what I call the "Doorway to Spirit" and take a person out of "consensus reality" and into the "shamanic state of consciousness."

Looking back, the ancient Greeks attributed sickness to *malaria* ("bad air") or unseen spiritual forces. The same idea is applied to sickness today by shamanic healers in the Amazon jungle (in Spanish, *aire malo*) and elsewhere. Shamans worldwide understand that all illness has an energetic component, because all physical life arises from the field of life energy many people call the *Source*.

When Western science discovered microbes in the 1600s, it began to understand disease as having mechanistic sources that could be cured through treatments like drugs and surgery. Science began to see "bad air" as superstition, whereas microbes were real. Yet, in every culture and time, people have had experiences with spirits and played witness to that duality. Over the past 100 years, studies across fields as diverse as quantum physics, anthropology, psychology, and human consciousness have taught us how malleable the definition of reality is and shown that there's room for both microbes *and* drums in our healing practices.

As the word *shaman* became generic in the Western world, many indigenous healing and spiritual practices were folded into it. Nowadays, the "shaman" is a healer, minister, spiritual teacher, herbalist, ceremony-maker, dream interpreter, therapist, destiny-revealer, astrologer, finder of what is lost, animal communicator, wisdom keeper, ghost chaser, and psychic. Suffice to say, it's a lot.

Perhaps an acceptable definition for "shaman" for this book can be "the worker (or walker) between the worlds," or, "the one who works with the unseen." The word may sound a little like a Tungusic word, but it doesn't have the same meaning, and our workers are not like Evenki/Tungus shamans of Siberia.

If those first European anthropologists had studied the Sámi people of northern Norway, our generic word might instead be *noadi* ("the one who sees in the dark," or as my Sámi teacher said, "the one who listens"). If they had traveled to Mongolia, our word today may have been *böge* (male shaman) or *idugan* (female shaman). If they had taken a boat to Laos and studied the Hmong hill tribes that had descended from China and Siberia before that, our word today might be *Shee Yee* (after the first shaman of the Hmong tradition) or *txiv neeb*, which means "the master of spirits." While we could have stumbled upon any one of thousands of words, it's helpful to remember that "shaman" is just a word.

The Connective Start of Shamanism

It is often stated that shamanism is humanity's first spiritual practice, the wellspring of all religions, and the oldest religion, being more than 50,000 years old. In Europe, the mysteriously elegant late Paleolithic cave paintings are commonly said to show evidence of shamanic practices dating back 35,000 years. In addition, petroglyphs and rock etchings linked to shamanism by theory are found throughout the world. Just looking at photographs of ancient rock art can fill you with awe and a sense that the artists were fueled by some type of religious or devotional impulse. Even so, no one truly knows what was in the mind of a cave painter or rock carver; artistic intention cannot be carbon-dated. But, if you think about how frightening it must have been to crawl long distances down narrow, pitch-dark tunnels in order to reach a cave chamber and then paint by torchlight, it seems likely something more than mere entertainment was urging the artists onward. That same raw force of yearning for contact, healing, and connection with the Great Mystery is in you, right now, or you would not be reading this book.

Shamanism and Animism Explained

There is a blurry relationship between *shamanism* and *animism*. *Anima* is Latin for soul, and the root for our word *animate*. The core of animism is that everything is alive (animated) with consciousness, essence, or spirit, and that humans can communicate with, and ask for help from, the spirits. Animists see the earth as a "giving environment." There are many animistic religions.

Shamanologists make an important distinction between animism and shamanism: All shamanists are animistic, but not all animists are shamanistic. A shamanic culture (or practice) has two unique characteristics:

The spirits have chosen (demanded) the human to become a shaman. This is no small burden, and, in tradition, those who are chosen by the spirits may suffer mightily, especially if they try to refuse the call.

The journey to the otherworld (the "soul-flight"). Once committed to following the call, the shaman learns how to embark on this journey through a trance state, often induced by sustained percussion.

While in the world of Spirit, the shaman is shown the diagnosis for illness and sees which treatments are needed to encourage healing. The treatment may involve negotiating directly with the spirit of the illness, or the rescue of a lost soul (shamanic cultures typically understand that humans have more than one soul). Regardless, healing in a shamanic sense may mean:

- calling back vital power that has been lost through some trauma

- tricking, feeding, or battling malevolent entities that are feeding on one's energy

- extracting spiritual intrusions in the body

- healing the ancestors who are intruding on the human world, causing illness

Treatment may involve creating a peace agreement between the seen and unseen worlds. The goal is to reset the chaos that emerges when the two worlds are in conflict—to restore the reciprocal, life-supporting balance between humans and the unseen powers that influence our lives. Because shamanism originally arose out of hunting cultures, creating peace between the worlds can involve repaying the spirit world (or the "Master of Animals") for the animals that humans must eat in order to live. When that debt, or other debts to the web of life, goes unpaid, the spirits may cause harm to us. (This is a specifically shamanic angle underlying the popular memes around "gratitude.")

Shamanologists tell us this history: Some 50,000 years ago, as small bands of animistic humans traveled in every direction out of the womb of Africa, they began to live different kinds of lives across landscapes in Europe, Central Asia, Southeast Asia, Australia, and, later, the Americas. In many places, these travelers interbred with the early-human inhabitants of the local landscapes. Perhaps 10,000 years ago, what we now call shamanism emerged in Central Asia. As migration is never-ceasing, specific shamanic practices disbursed in all directions, to places such as Korea, Southeast Asia, Finland, Hungary, Alaska, Greenland, and the Northwest coast of North America. Shamanic knowledge reached into the most remote points of the globe, including far-flung areas of the Amazon jungle and a few of the over 500 North American tribes.

It is a popular idea that shamans are loved and revered as wise elders and magnificent teachers of the ways of Spirit—ones who know unseen mysteries and possess powers beyond our grasp. This is frequently true, and it springs from the shaman's intense, rigorous, and often extraordinary suffering-filled training that expands their vision of reality, widens their humanity, and refines their compassion. However, it is also true that shamans are sometimes viewed with fear, suspicion, and envy for the same reasons. Shamans are regularly blamed for anything strange or negative happening in a village, and sometimes killed for it. The life of a shaman can be lonely because of its acute strangeness, often bordering on (or crossing over into) madness.

The modern word, *shaman,* is an ungainly word to be sure, because it is trying to capture an understanding of life that

Western, rational, monotheistic culture has tried to abolish: an ensouled earth, the existence of helpers from layers of reality that cannot be measured by the senses or scientific devices, the ability of the soul to travel between realms, and the energetic (not merely chemical) healing powers found throughout nature.

Shamanism has spread throughout the world for 10,000 years, evolving every step along the way. That is still true today, as shamanic practices continue to spread and evolve. By reading this book and familiarizing yourself with shamanic techniques, you are part of that continuing evolution, in your landscape, in your time.

A WORLD OF SHAMANISM

Shamanism in Central Asia (1)

Central Asia (e.g., Siberia and Mongolia) is commonly recognized as the birthplace of shamanism. Many core practices of shamanism across the globe can be traced back to migrations out of this area.

In modern times, we focus on shamanism as a healing practice, but its origins begin in hunting cultures in Central Asia. Early shamans may very well have seen the obtaining of animals in the hunt as more fundamental than healing, as the primary role of the ancient Asiatic shaman was to be "the one who knows" where the animals were. Failure to lead hunters to prey had significant repercussions. If the hunts were unsuccessful, starvation could result. "Searching and finding," therefore, is a core practice in shamanism. This activity is reflected in some of the healing practices where the shaman searches for a lost soul, finds it, and returns it to the patient's body.

By coming into intimate contact with the Master Spirit of the hunted animals, the shaman ensured the survival of the people. By making the proper ceremonies to the animal spirits and offering tea, milk, or alcohol as repayment for the lives of animals taken, the shaman helped the killed animals travel safely to the afterlife. By ensuring the tribe followed strict ethical rules, such as not taking more than needed and making sure the animals were properly honored, shamans maintained balance and respect between the two worlds. Achieving harmony between the realms was critical for a shaman of hunting communities. Without it, continued abundance (animals) for his or her people could not be guaranteed.

Shamanism in Mongolia (2)

There is a relationship between the Mongolian shaman's drum and the horse. Shamans-in-training were given a wooden staff with a horse's head carved on it. When they had gained enough

skill and power, which comes from direct relationship with the helping spirits, the staff was replaced with a drum that was typically made from horsehide. The shaman's drum probably originated in Central Asia, and it is commonly believed that horses were first domesticated in the China/Mongolia region some 6,000 years ago.

Mongolian shamans—and many shamans since—viewed the drum as their "spirit horse" upon which they swiftly rode to the spirit world, often to the upper realms just above the mountains where the powerful sky spirit and primordial shamans live. The name for the wild horses that once roamed Mongolia is *takhi*, which also means "spirit" or "spiritual."

Shamanism in Siberia (3)

If we go north from Mongolia, across the dramatic Altai Mountains and into subarctic Russia and Siberia, we meet the "reindeer herding people." Like other shamans, they, too, use drums as a vital part of their practice. Frequently the drums are made from reindeer hide, as reindeer are the shaman's primary helper. To the people of this area, reindeer are viewed as "the protecting and sustaining mother of life."

The relationship between Siberian shamans and reindeer gives you an idea of how integrated shamanic practice is with the animals, plants, minerals, and land in the immediate landscape. Worldwide, the core idea of shamanism is that direct contact with the local land—with *essence, source, life force of all creation*—can fill you with raw power, and that power can be used for healing or divining.

Simple objects like a stone, bone, antler, or feather are packed with the raw energy of nature and can be used as a transmitter of that power. This is what the young Mongolian's staff and, later, the drum can do. These tools can be used to open the doorway to Spirit and transmit *source* energy (including the shaman's "free soul" in flight) to the world of *essence*.

Shamanism in China and Southeast Asia (4)

Moving south from Mongolia into China, Tibet, the Himalayas, Korea, and Southeast Asia, we see that ancient shamanic practices mingled with Tantrism (~400 CE) and Buddhism (~700 CE) over time, blurring the line between shamanism and these newer religions. Tibetan Buddhist priests work with the same spirits of the land to do the same healings as shamans but

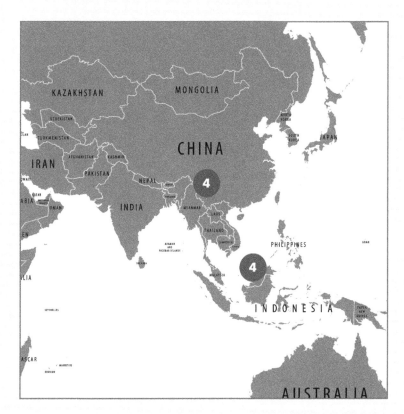

refer to the spirits as "the primal five elements." The gong and finger cymbals, central to Buddhism, became a shaman's tool for summoning helping spirits, and the ritual garb of the tribal shaman was slowly replaced by formalized attire that echoed priestly robes from those religions.

Shamanism in Australia and New Zealand (5)

In these vast island landscapes, shamanic practice is closely tied to the energy lines running through the land, and to the "time before and outside of time." In this "Dreamtime," heroic ancestor spirits, who are part human (in their emotions) and part mammal, bird, or reptile (in physical shape), formed the world along with all of the life-forms and moral laws that humans must follow. In some stories, after they set all things into their visible shapes, the ancestors disappeared into the crevices of the earth, and the winds and waters, and became what we now call the "natural forces." The Dreamtime is actually not in the past, but the "always," the "everywhen."

The Dreamtime ancestors place a claim and a responsibility on families or clans by becoming their totem. That human group is responsible for the stewardship of their totem, which may take the form of an animal, plant, or spot of land.

A person's totem—their guiding spirit or helper spirit—can be a lake near where they were born, or an animal or plant that has a special relationship with their kin's ancestral line. It's a good thing to remember the landscape of your birth and ask whether you feel a special energetic relationship to it or support from it. Or through meditation, you can see whether your family seems to have a relationship with a certain animal. These are some ways that shamans of Oceania identified their totems or spirit helpers.

The traditional healers of central Australia are called *ngangkari*. Like shamans everywhere, they understand that pain, disease, and illness are linked to an imbalance in the spirit. They often describe the healing "power" coming to them without asking for it, or being transmitted to them by a parent.

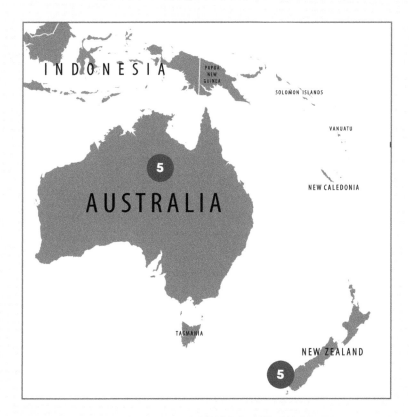

The power gives them the ability to hear and see through the physical layer of the body and into the spiritual depths below, where they can, through "strong touch," pull illness or pain out and throw it away. The refinement of this power is the life's work of these shamans. Like other shamanic healers, they tap into the "source" (which has called them into this service) and channel its powers into the physical work in this world. The power of "everywhen" flows into and through them in order to bring healing in the physical world.

Shamanism in Europe (6)

Like Buddhism and Tantrism in Asia, European Christianity came into contact with older indigenous traditions. As the two practices interacted, they often overlapped. Churches were constructed on spots of significance to indigenous peoples, transmuting ancient spirit-deities into Christian saints. The elements of indigenous belief that Christianity could not absorb met much more severe pushback, and the church tried to abolish or obliterate spiritual practices that were incongruous. During the "witch burning times" between the 15th and 17th centuries, the majority of witches executed were simply rural herbal healers, many of them genuinely shamanic.

The witch's broomstick is similar to the shaman's drum or staff in that it serves as a kind of vehicle to carry the practitioner to the otherworld. In a Nordic tradition called "staving," women often strike a larger staff with a smaller stick and sing trance-inducing songs. A witch may or may not have been

"called" to work with the spirits in the same exact way as an Asiatic shaman, but witches have similar relationships with spirit helpers and an understanding of reciprocity between the seen and unseen. Hallucinogenic or vision-expanding plants were also a part of European tradition, including "flying ointment," which was made from certain plants said to help witches travel to the spirit world.

The ancient Greeks had numerous titles and monikers for healers that indicate the presence of shamanic practices. The *iatromantis*, for example, was said to make trance-induced journeys into other dimensions and return with esoteric information. Many orgiastic (trance-induced) cult rites like the famous "Eleusinian Mysteries" peppered the Hellenic landscape for centuries before the arrival of Christianity. Many of these rituals were associated with far older practices that placated or honored the Master of Animals or Lady of the Wild Things—the spirits of earth that made food available to human beings.

In northern Scandinavia, the indigenous Sámi people retain shamanistic practices that clearly relate to the ancient Siberian ways. The shaman's drum is typically made of reindeer hide, and a reindeer antler is used as a drumstick. The Sámi use a powerful type of ritual singing called *joiking* (pronounced YOI-king) to honor the helping spirits of nature and entice their helping spirits to cooperate in healing. Some Sámi make regular offerings to the revered forest god Laib olmai, another form of the Master of Animals.

Many elements of pre-Christian religion are clearly shamanic, including the central image of the world tree (discussed later on page 130) from which the archetypal god of Nordic shamanism, Odin, hangs upside down for nine days, sacrificing one eye in order to become "one who sees" into the other world.

A fascinating example of European shamanism can be found in 16th-century Italy. As witch trials were common then, many stories started to emerge that shared strange commonalities. Italians of the time reported that they had been compelled by the spirits to become *benandanti* ("good walkers"), whose job was to leave their bodies at night and meet with other good walkers in the fields outside of town to do battle with malev-olent witches who were bent on poisoning or destroying the crops. One would become a benandanti for a certain number of years and then be released from the obligation. In a night-marish irony, the priest-judges of the Inquisition came to believe the benandanti to be witches themselves and ultimately executed many.

Perhaps the best-known example of European shamanism is the Celtic world. Druids were the intellectual leaders of their place and time, and combined the roles of priest, judge, healer, scholar, and teacher. Whether druids entered trances and jour-neyed to the spirit world is a topic of intense debate. However, hallucinogenic mushrooms such as *Psilocybe cyanescens* (wavy caps) that were elemental in shamanic practices can be found growing all across the British Isles. It is nearly impossi-ble to believe that druids never used these powerful spiritual helpers. One of the central parts of an Irish bardic poet's years of training involved seclusion in a dark chamber and "eating of the sacred flesh" in order to receive visions from the spirits. Irish and Scottish texts are profuse with spells and charms for healing with the aid of the spirits of nature. Moreover, the Celtic tradition is rife with stories of journeys into the faerie realm. These trips often took seekers down into the green hills to a magical lower world of wisdom and healing (as well as never-ending feasting, dancing, and fornication).

In the Celtic world, we again meet the Master of Animals, this time called *Cernunnos*, an antlered god who calls the animals to be hunted. Echoing the Aboriginal Australian story of the world-creating ancestors who, after assembling the visible world, sunk into the in-between places of the earth, winds, and seas, the Celtic gods, too, vanished into the green faerie mounds after the modern humans appeared on the land, *becoming* the forces of nature.

There is an intriguing Celtic tradition that's still alive, though only barely. "Sin eating," a practice that has strong shamanic roots, is the ritual act of placing a plate of food from the wake upon the coffin of the recently deceased (in some practices, the plate is placed directly on the dead person's belly). The wake is a joyous event until the arrival of the sin eater, who begins to eat the food atop the dead person as a way of extracting the sin from the person's life. The concept is that the deceased, unburdened of their sins and negative energetic weight, will be able to enter the next world in peace.

Shamanism in South America (7)

About 25,000 years ago, the ancestors of First Nations people of North and South America split off from their Siberian home and slowly made their way across the land bridge connecting Siberia and Alaska. These groups carried with them the shamanic practices that arose in Asia.

When they arrived in North America, they split into two now genetically distinct groups. One spread across North America, and the other moved south, becoming the ancestors to Central and South Americans about 14,000 years ago.

The shaman is a dominant presence throughout South America. The use of hallucinogenic plants is more pronounced there than anywhere in the world, but it should be noted that not all shamans use hallucinogens. Some shamans focus on singing magical chants that call spirits to work with them, and the healing is done through singing. Also the line between shamans and sorcerers is the thinnest in South America, and sometimes the terms for both are the same.

In South America, there is a well-known energy called *envidia,* which means "envy." Envidia also has a broader meaning of wishing ill upon someone who has more luck or abundance than you do. Instead of attending to your own life, you reach out with blame. Healers spend a great deal of time cleansing envidia that has been placed on someone, either by someone else or by a hired sorcerer.

About 8,000 years ago, a dramatic influence arrived in much of South American shamanism: the use of psychotropic plants, including the wide cultivation of tobacco. Considered by many shamans to be the most powerful healing plant of all, tobacco fundamentally altered many of the shamanic practices across the continent, particularly the humid western half of South America where it can be grown.

Tobacco has many medicinal uses, particularly as an insect repellant (tobacco juice rubbed on the skin) and, when drunk in larger doses, it is an excellent vermifuge, causing intense vomiting that expels worms and parasites. Tobacco also has some hallucinogenic capacities when taken in certain ways (and proper doses), including smoking it, drinking tobacco juice, snuffing it, and using it as a suppository. For *curanderos* (the Spanish word for "folk healer"), tobacco carries the power of purification and sanctification, and it is used constantly in healing and ritual work. Tobacco clears negative energy from a person, protects them against malevolent spirits, and opens channels for Spirit to enter.

In many jungle traditions of South America, it is common for a shaman to conduct a *dieta*—a prolonged ceremony (seven days or often much longer) of fasting, prayer, and ingesting a single plant in order to build their shamanic power. In this work, the shaman marries the plant spirit in their energetic body, and the plant is then always present as a healing ally. The plants help the shaman build power in their bellies, sometimes called *mariri* or *yachay.* This power can be used to send energy outward as healing.

I have completed *dietas* of six different Amazonian plants in my studies (including tobacco). Working deeply with the plant spirits in this way has infused me with a kind of "knowing" that is very different from the intellectual knowledge that the Western mind claims as the only true knowing. For me, the human intellect tends to separate and compare or contrast, always asking for "more." Plant consciousness is more about harmonizing and collaborating; the plants teach us to seek "right relationship" with the world, and to place our attention on seeking "enough."

West of the Amazon basin, the Andes Mountains slither like a giant serpent along the western edge of South America. With their snow-capped peaks, the landscape is radically different from the jungle, but some of the core practices of shamanism are here, too. For example, the idea of the "three-tiered cosmos" of upper, middle, and lower worlds (page 130) is prevalent in the Andean world.

In the jungle, the curanderos call on the spirits of the plants and animals that carry so much power. In the high places, the *paqos* ask the plants and animals for help, but they also call on the *apus* (pronounced AH-poos)—the mountain spirits. A paqo may encounter an apu in a dream or trance-induced ceremony, and the apu may show itself as an animal (perhaps a hummingbird, condor, puma, or bull) or as a radiant human being. When an apu comes to someone, it instills in them a power, called an *estrella* (meaning "star"), that helps the paqo heal. (This experience actually came to me during a nighttime vigil with Apu Waqaywillka in Peru. I also witnessed my Andean teacher commune with his apus as he conducted a healing on a young man.)

A common idea in shamanism is that the landscape of your birth, or a powerful landscape you feel very connected to, may be an energetic portal for you. It may be the portal through which you came from the world of Spirit and into physical form. In the Andean tradition, this is sometimes called the *itu,* a natural formation like a rock, lake, river, or mountain. This idea extends to include other "power spots" that can be a doorway through which you receive blessings from Spirit. This is a fundamental idea in shamanism worldwide, and one we'll delve into even more later on.

Shamanism in North America (8)

Within the United States, there are 562 First Nation tribes. Among them is a wide array of beliefs, languages, and customs. Like everywhere on earth, some tribes are more classically shamanic while others are more classically animistic.

Among the Ojibwa, Innu, Cree, Penobscot, and Abenaki is the ceremony of the shaking tent, which is performed to induce spiritual healing. The healer is placed inside a special tent or lodge. His hands are tied behind him, and his body is wrapped tightly in a blanket. For the Lakota, this is the *yuwipi* ceremony, and it is steered by the yuwipi *wicaša*, or yuwipi man. In Lakota, *yuwipi* means "they wrap him up." As the yuwipi man calls out to the spirits, the entire structure shakes violently, and the yuwipi man, as well as those gathered, see and speak with the spirits that arrive. Western medicine may cure what the Lakota call "white sickness," but only the yuwipi man can heal the sickness caused by disharmony between humans and the spirit world. The yuwipi man gives up part of his life each time he performs the ceremony in order to serve his people. (If you begin doing healing work on other people, you may well want to ask Spirit what your agreement is. What price are you willing to pay for being a healer?)

For the Kiowa of Colorado, a similar shaking tent ceremony involves the Owl Doctor invoking the Owl Spirit—a rather

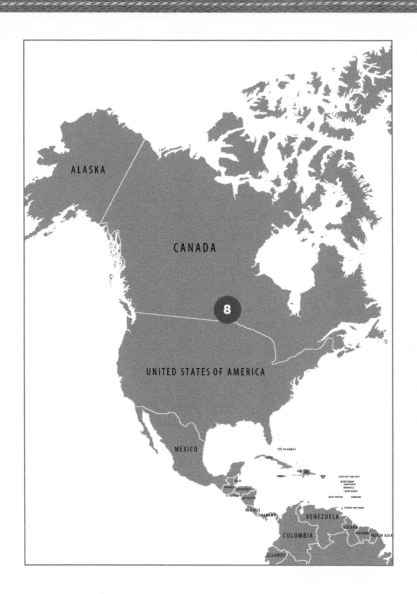

dangerous ambassador of the powers of death and wisdom—
to descend into the tent to help in healing and divination.

In the Southern United States and portions of Mexico and
Central America, the use of peyote, an entheogen cactus, and
various species of "magic" mushrooms are used ceremonially
for healing. The Mazatec ceremony of the *velada* (Spanish for
"evening") is led by a *chota chjine,* or "person of wisdom,"
who sings, dances, and allows the mushroom spirits to speak
through them. They also perform direct healing on those present, sometimes sucking out "bad air" or malevolent energies
from someone's body in what is called an "extraction." This is
a dangerous type of healing that should be conducted only by
well-trained healers.

About Cultural Appropriation

If you are a citizen of the "dominant culture" anywhere on earth, you are likely living on land from which indigenous people were displaced violently. You've seen me mention elsewhere in this chapter how critically important the local land is in indigenous and shamanistic thinking. For most industrial-age citizens, especially those living in urban centers, it is nearly impossible to comprehend this connection to the local land as a living spiritual force that feeds your essential life power and that you also feed in return. Loving your city or having pride in your town is not at all the same thing.

The "industrial machine mind" that rules the modern world has no concept of the problem with paving over a grove of trees or diverting a stream in order to build something important—for "progress." But the "indigenous soul" cries out, and that wound is not easily healed, because it is a wound to the soul of both the land and the inhabitants of that land.

Many First Nations people worldwide see that the only thing that has not been taken from them are their spiritual traditions (and, in America, they were forbidden by law to practice those until 1978). Western capitalism and indigenous spirituality are seen by many as completely incongruent. The idea of selling ritual items, or charging money upfront for healing work, is frequently seen as deeply offensive to First Nation people. How can anyone work shamanically with integrity while having to survive inside a capitalistic system? This is a very thorny issue. All of this inspires many First Nations people to see the genocide as not happening in the past, but as ongoing.

The entire issue of appropriation is made more complex by the fact that many indigenous peoples' own traditions are vanishing as their young people lose interest in the old ways. Some indigenous healers are grateful that urban Westerners want to be trained in shamanism. And the swelling interest among those city-dwelling, non-indigenous people emerges from the wrenching loss that they feel, perhaps in their own inborn indigenous soul, of what the machine mind has stolen from them, scores of generations before they were born. Questions of "who can own healing practices?" or "who can Spirit choose to work with?" arise, with no clear answer.

The easiest way to avoid cultural appropriation is to take your spiritual yearning and dive into your own ethnic history. Shamanism is global; somewhere in your genes, in the "every-when" Dreamtime where your primordial ancestors still live, your own shamanic tradition lives. Dive into your own ancestral lines. Of course, this is part of the complexity, because most people have many genetic ancestral lines operating in them simultaneously. If you do choose to delve into an ethnically specific shamanic tradition, the best advice I can offer is to study with a living indigenous elder who has been raised in that tradition, submit to their instruction, and continually ask their permission to take the next step. Also, to the degree possible, learn the language. Every culture's cosmology is buried in the language.

If you feel called to study culturally specific shamanic practices that are not from your own ancestral lines:

Study respectfully with an indigenous elder from that tradition. Follow their lead. Seek their permission. Listen, listen, listen.

Learn (as much as possible) the native language. The shamanic mind of a culture is embedded in its language.

Approach the study with "a certain difficult repentance" as the poet D. H. Lawrence said. Studying shamanic ways will not evaporate your connection to a tragic history, but humility and a difficult repentance may help you become one drop in the ocean of healing.

Ask yourself what you can do with your privilege that you are not doing now that is in alignment with your stated spiritual framework. (And ask where in your life you are living a lie that you can stop living.)

Listen to those who challenge or criticize, because this issue is deep, real, and full of pain. Respect the feedback you are given.

Know that every true spiritual path is difficult. Ask Spirit to continue to clean your heart and clear your mind, and give you courage to tell, and live, the truth.

Finally, like everything on earth, words carry power. Calling a Native American medicine person, elder, or spiritual master a shaman is seen as a sign of cultural illiteracy and an act of diminishing their specific status—on par with calling a Catholic priest a yogi. However, because the term has become generic, some indigenous people do use it as shorthand when they are communicating with Western urban people about their spiritual practices. If you study and begin to practice shamanic healing techniques, the most accurate, common, and widely accepted term to refer to yourself that's meant to alleviate some issues of cultural appropriation is *shamanic practitioner*.

In short, don't call yourself a shaman.

Conclusion: From Spoken Word to True Techniques

Shamanism has always been passed down orally from elder teacher to eager student. There is no official scripture unless it is life itself, and the land itself. There is no dogma unless it is "be fully alive, be well, and be in right relationship to all creatures." Like the land itself, shamanic ideas and practices shift over time. And, yet, there are threads that connect the disparate shamanic and animistic cultures to one another through time:

- For shamans, loyalty to Earth as a "giving environment" is paramount.

- While life has plenty of fear, under all fear is awe and wonder.

- Shamans everywhere recognize their responsibility to both past and future generations.

- Finally, even the best shamans have a fundamental humility regarding their place, and humanity's place, in the order of things.

The fabric of global shamanism is woven of certain practices and techniques used for coming into powerful relationship with the Spirit of Creation, powers that help some people learn to be healers. In the next chapter, we will begin to explore some of those most common and enduring techniques.

Chapter 2

Shamanic Techniques of Ecstasy

As we'll explore in this chapter, there are many ways to delve into how the shaman heals—from percussive music to vocally driven chants and songs, meditative and visualization practices, and methods to manipulate and challenge the body, psyche, and mind. Standing strongly amongst those tools is the use of trance work, and there are many paths to get there.

The Healing Pathways of Trance

A shaman's healing work is performed in some kind of a trance state, altered perception, or expanded consciousness. The difference between trance and "deep meditation" is that trance involves rhythm. A trance state is created physically by the shift of brain wave patterns brought on by sustained rhythm, and emotionally by the clear, passionate intention of prayer that the shaman utters. The most critical goal of the trance state is to "let go of your self-importance." In the trance state, shamans call their spirit helpers to them and connect themselves to their healing powers and to the *source* of all power. In certain circumstances their "free soul" leaves what we call "reality" (or this plane of it) and travels to the spirit world (what we may call a level of consciousness different from the ordinary). Shamans attain the trance state through a wide variety of these rhythmic "techniques of ecstasy."

Sacred Drumming

If you listen to any sustained rhythm long enough, like a drum, rattle, sticks, or even a washing machine or clothes dryer, it will induce some kind of trance. When we hear drumming at a certain monotonous pace, our brain waves begin to match (or "entrain") the wave pattern, slowing from faster beta waves to alpha waves. In a trance state, our breathing slows and deepens. When fully entranced, we relax more. As the trance deepens, we enter the theta wave-state, where waves that are present in that twilight place between waking and sleeping are more pronounced.

Drumming mysteriously connects us deeply to the life force coursing through everything. As we fall deeper into the trance, the pace of theta brain waves connects us to the foundational

hum of Earth, the universe, and creation itself. Whether or not that is true scientifically, there is no doubt about the effect a repeating drum beat has. As we fall deeper into the trance, our brain waves slow, prompting us to open ourselves and loosen our grip on the ego. As this happens, the body begins to feel light, and images may begin to appear in the mind's eye. As the trance progresses, we enter a liminal space where the line between the conscious and the unconscious blurs. This happens as we approach the "Doorway to Spirit." When we enter this state carrying an intention—a prayer—that doorway may very well swing open and bring us teaching or healing.

Our lives are also deeply impacted by the greater rhythms of the universe around us. Cyclical movements like the sun and moon rising and falling, the flow of one season to the next, the circular dance of the earth around the sun, and even the shrinking and expansion of the universe all impact how we live from moment to moment. Shamanic percussion (whether with drum, gong, sticks, or shakers) takes us to this place that is at once as big as the universe and as small as a neuron or atom, where we may ask politely for the door to Spirit to swing open and bring help.

Chanting and Singing

Singing is breath with intention infused into it, and breath is the primal element of air flowing through us. Air is the most ephemeral of the four classic elements (air, fire, water, earth). This is why breath is, across cultures, associated with Spirit. While we open our body only a few times per day for food and water, each day we take in air 23,000 times.

Different kinds of breathing techniques are integral, and shamans have employed deep, rapid, or elongated breathing to induce trances and even visions. All singing is a kind of breathwork, and that work varies based on the desired intention. Some songs require deep, fast breaths, whereas others need slower, elongated ones. Shamanic singing incorporates more than just breath; the beauty of melody and the intention of words are equally incorporated into the song.

Shamans understand singing as a way of transmuting energy and then transmitting or transferring it. A prayer or intention is a kind of diaphanous *physical* energy—a vibrational wave pattern—infused into the song that, like a wagon, carries the prayer through the air and into a person's body. A prayer for cleansing has a slightly different wave pattern than a prayer for abundance, or one for protection. This is, admittedly, very subtle, and pinpoints what shamanic training is for.

My teachers in Peru place the vibrational pattern of a healing plant onto their ritual song, and that song carries the power of that plant into the body of the patient. The same can be done by asking the vibrational pattern of an animal, or the sun, for example, to be carried by the song. That song enters the the patient's physical body. There it enters their physical and energetic body to bring about healing. This is the difference between shamanism and other spiritual singing. Shamanic singing is not abstract, intellectual, or theological; it is like handing someone a plate of food or drink of water. The song itself functions as medicine.

Science has shown that the largest electromagnetic field in the body is generated by the heart. In fact, using an electroencephalogram, we can see that the output from the heart is 60 times greater in amplitude than that of brain waves. Researchers found that a transference of that electromagnetic energy can happen between two people who are in close proximity. Shamanic healing songs work on a similar basis. The vibration of the voice and breath are the physical carrier of the energy, and the intention, prayer, or shaman's power are the medicine.

THE SHAMANIC HEALING SONG

A shamanic healing song can be exceedingly simple in melody and words. The healing power is not totally in the words, melody, or performance; it is an infusion of spiritual medicine. The power of the song is in your heart—in its sincere yearning to heal yourself, another person, the land, or the world—and in your unobstructed connection to Spirit.

Think of any two notes and use them for this song. Experiment with different pairs of notes and see how it feels to you for this song. I'll mark them as #1 and #2 on page 39. Make the first note lower than the second note, and then try it reversed to see what the power is like for you. This healing song calls on natural powers to deliver their specific kind of energy for healing. Everything in the universe has its own vibration, its own song, its own power.

Begin your song by taking a moment to ask Spirit to open and cleanse you, fill you with love, and make you able to summon and transmit this healing energy. Focus on what needs healing applied to it. Open. Let whatever image from nature pop into your head and then sing it. Sing in as many powers as are needed for this healing (sun, moon, water, deer, salmon, bee, daisy—on and on).

1	2	1	2
Po-	wer of the river,	po-	wer of the river
1	2	1	2
Br-	ing your healing,	br-	ing your healing.

(Repeat at least once, or several times, before calling in another "helper.")

The word *power* can be replaced with *spirit* or *love* or whatever seems right. You can also use the Spanish verb *cura* (pronounced *KOO-ruh*) repeated four times to replace the entire second line. It means "to heal." If you find as you sing the song that the melody begins to shift and you add more notes, that's great! Let the song become what it wants to become.

Ecstatic Dancing

Shamans use dancing to call and open power to themselves, to create sacred space around a ceremony, to move themselves (and others) into an expanded consciousness where they can do their healing work, or to honor a spirit guide or power animal. Sometimes dancing is a way of lending one's body to a spirit who does not have a body. While they are dancing through the shaman's body, the spirit may bring a different, larger power and sight to the shaman, and they can then transmit it to the patient. Sometimes ecstatic dance prepares the shaman for the journey to the spirit world. They dance for minutes, hours, or even days until, exhausted and totally open and ready, they lie down and their soul flies to the spirit world to begin the work of healing.

The word *ecstasy* means to "stand outside oneself" or "to leave." Dancing is a fast and effective way to access trance energies, especially if the dancer goes beyond their usual comfort zone. Shamans across time have used dancing as a way to "get out of their own way," to leave the constraints of the rational, logical mind and become open to the help of Spirit or the spirits. Dancing is frequently accompanied by drumming and chanting.

When it comes to "leaving the body," curiously, the way out is in. When you dance deeply, discarding self-judgment and completely exiting any thought of what you look like, this is a form of ecstasy. By going deeply into the body as a vehicle for pure prayer, and by letting Spirit dance *you*, you exit the world of human rules and enter the world of Spirit. Dancing is moving prayer; it's a prayer set in motion. Your sweat becomes an offering to Spirit, a form of holy water for the gods.

Fasting

All trance is about exiting a smaller power (the rational mind, or "the expectations of others") and opening to the larger power (the supra-rational mind or Spirit). The trance state can be opened by exhausting the body, as with dancing, by disrupting the body's natural needs and rhythms, or by depriving the body of what it needs to continue its normal operations. Trance is always about exiting the normal or "consensus reality" and entering what at once is a larger, more deeply personal and private reality.

Like all shamanic practices (and, really, everything else) there are degrees of fasting. You could fast for a few hours or days from all food. You could fast from most food for a very long time, taking in only the bare minimum to keep the door to death closed. Or, like the tradition of Lent in Catholicism, you can fast from a specific *kind* of food, or from a certain habitual behavior. Different types of fasting can be used to achieve desired results.

Among many tribes in the Amazon jungle, including my teachers from the Shipibo people, shamans in training enter into a ceremonial process called a *dieta* in which they eat only a small bit of grilled fish and rice once a day for many days, sometimes for more than a year, while they focus their body's attention on ingesting a single plant that brings them certain powers. This limited fasting opens the energy channels in their body to make room to receive the teachings and the power of the plant as it merges with their energetic signature. In many shamanic traditions, total fasting for several days in a row is a way to tear down all internal obstacles between the person and Spirit, and this kind of fast is used for huge intimations into a different kind of life—like "wiping" a computer of accumulated data and starting new, or like constructing a whole new floor of the psyche.

Like all the other shamanic practices, fasting is about much more than meets the eye. To fast means more than simply restricting material intake or limiting the amount or type of nutrients and chemicals entering the body. Fasting is prayer. It is an offering made to Spirit—an opportunity to formally demonstrate one's seriousness on the path and willingness to break down inner barriers so as to be transformed by Spirit. It is an act of pleading with Spirit to cleanse the barriers to wisdom. The individual who is fasting sacrifices the body's "lower," more immediate needs and replaces them with a "higher desire"—for communion with Spirit.

Fasting can be dangerous. Do not do dramatic fasts without guidance from a knowledgeable teacher, as well as a consultation with medical professionals. If you have any medical issues or problems, be careful when experimenting with even the most minimal fasting.

Vigils and Meditations

A vigil is a form of fasting from sleep. During the vigil, you enter a state of devotion and prayer and maintain wakefulness. Staying awake can bring on a trance state, and adding in prayer and intention can open a potent state of being "in-between" the worlds of waking and dreaming. Vigils are acts of devotion. They demonstrate to Spirit (and to yourself) that you are willing to enter into discomfort in order to receive wisdom, teaching, power, or healing. Like all other practices, your intention is the key.

Often the intention for a vigil has a specific focus. Shamans might enter a vigil outside, staying awake all night to greet the dawn, making prayers to help them or someone else enter a new life, or transform. Another example could be a vigil for the ancestors performed at Halloween—what the Celtic and Wiccan traditions call Samhain (pronounced *SOW-wen*)—when the veil between the living and dead is thinnest.

Vigils intend to make you *vigilant* toward something—an issue, a landscape, a person, a deity, an intention. You stay awake through the "dark night of the soul" battling the powers of the night and the body that try to urge you to relent and give in, to give up on this long prayer you are making. When the dawn comes and you have succeeded, it can bring a burst of great joy—another common definition of "ecstasy."

Meditation is a broad term, and I'd like to highlight a difference I see between traditional meditation (called "mindfulness meditation") and shamanic meditation. Classic mindfulness meditation is a process of *emptying* your mind of the stream of thoughts that try to command your attention and force emotional reactions. A shamanic meditation, however, may be called a prolonged visualization of inviting power into the body, which often arrives as imagery or emotions.

An example of shamanic meditation is the practice of visualizing your breath carrying the power of the rising sun into your body on the inhale. Once inside, the solar power reaches throughout your body to collect any negative energy (anger, resentment, pain, envy, arrogance, shame, martyrdom, impatience), gathers that energy, and then carries it out of your body on the exhale. Another example is drawing a connection of energy between your heart center and any part of nature, like the sun, a river, a mountain, the wind, the earth under your house, ice, trees, flowers—on and on, and holding those lines of connection in your mind, seeing energy flowing from them to you and love flowing from you to them. Doing such a meditation for even 10 minutes can have palpable healing effects. Nature is eager to help us!

The Ins and Outs of Entheogens

The word *entheogen* comes from the Greek roots *gen* ("to become or create," like *genesis*) and *theo* (meaning "god"). Put together, the word means "becoming (or manifesting) god within oneself." For thousands of years, humans have been in contact with plants that, when ingested, open inner channels to direct experiences with forces greater than our ordinary consciousness allows in. Entheogen is a more useful word than hallucinogen, because it acknowledges and honors the spiritual component of these psychoactive substances.

Shamans understand that, as a "giving environment," Mother Earth serves up uncountable pathways for humans to "stand outside themselves" and draw in the immense powers of creation to open their contact with wonder, awe, beauty, and love. The sunset, the glitter of light on water, the sound of bees' wings, the drum and rattle, the touch on the skin—Mother Earth offers us an overflowing banquet of ways to infuse into ourselves the "wonder of having been created." Hallucinogenic plants are part of that immense banquet.

Entheogens like ayahuasca (South America), ibogaine (Africa), peyote (Mexico), and psilocybin mushrooms (everywhere!) carry a great deal of allure and fear. This fear has been compounded somewhat and, because of the Internet and the vast powers of spiritual consumerism, a plethora of misinformation is now available on the subject. The less dramatic stories of experiences with entheogens, which are far more common, don't get published.

These plant teachers and healers can, indeed, be incredibly powerful and deliver profound experiences of healing and insight. Many of the stories of rapid healing of old traumas, psychological patterns, and addictions are certainly true. Entheogens are not physically addictive like opioids are.

This doesn't mean entheogens are safe and benevolent. Like any tool—a hammer, electric saw, or a blender—entheogens are as safe as the person who is using them is smart, and, like anything that humans do on earth, the recipe for a bad time always includes ignorance, arrogance, fantasy, and greed.

Because the plants are powerful healers with a broad vision, they may determine that the healing or insight you need may be through discomfort. For example, a very common part of using some entheogens is vomiting, diarrhea, uncontrollable trembling, pain in the body, or weeping. On a spiritual level, these are ways to shake loose and release stored negative energies. People who think using plant medicine will give them a great pleasurable high that will instantly transform their old habits are in for a rough ride. My single bit of advice is to seek a teacher who is completely trustworthy, well-trained, and experienced at working with plant medicines. Consult a well-trained teacher, as well as your chosen medical professionals, before embarking upon any plant medicine work.

A BRIEF LIST OF ENTHEOGENS

Let's explore some of the world's entheogens most commonly used by shamanic practitioners, along with some of their entrancing properties and the flip side of their dangers. Though they are immensely well-known, you won't see synthetic hallucinogens like LSD and MDMA, or cannabis, which is classified as a mood-altering substance, but not a hallucinogen. It is important to note that, for many indigenous people, the use of entheogens is not primarily about seeking visions, but about facilitating the healing of illness.

PSILOCYBIN MUSHROOMS

There are over 100 species of mushrooms that contain psilocybin. They're widespread, growing on every continent except Antarctica, and some anthropologists posit that mushrooms are why humans evolved from a spiritual standpoint. Ingesting psilocybin impacts a user's emotional state in a number of different ways, and one might feel euphoric or experience a spike in empathy or atypical thinking. In some species, psilocybin can promote visuals whether one's eyes are closed or open. Mushrooms may be the gentlest of the plant medicines, since they rarely induce vomiting, though nausea may occur.

DMT/AYAHUASCA

While it's impossible to specify exactly, we know that N,N-dimethyltryptamine (DMT) has long been a tool among the more than 110 tribes of the northwestern region of the Amazon Basin where Colombia, Peru, Ecuador, and Brazil come together. Ayahuasca is one of the most potent psychedelic drugs on the planet, and ingesting this powerful, sacred substance can produce vibrant and strong hallucinations. Along with profound visuals, consuming ayahuasca also frequently results in vomiting, diarrhea, and overall bodily pain.

MESCALINE/PEYOTE

A psychedelic alkaloid native in both North and South American cacti, mescaline and peyote have long been a tool among the more than 110 tribes of the northwestern region of the Amazon basin where Colombia, Peru, Ecuador, and Brazil come together.

Peyote and mescaline users often experience deep, profound epiphanies while under the influence of the drug. Bitter tasting, peyote can cause users to experience nausea and vomiting.

IBOGAINE

A plant native to West Africa, ibogaine has a place of prominence in many tribal rituals. Recently, it has shown promise as a treatment for addiction and depression (as have other entheogens). Ibogaine can stimulate introspection and some euphoria but is also accompanied by effects like nausea and vomiting and may also have potentially negative effects upon the heart.

SALVIA DIVINORUM

Cultivated in the high ele-
vations of Oaxaca, Mexico,
salvinorin A, or "diviner's
sage," often elicits a feeling of detachment in those
who consume it. Frequently,
sensory stimuli like sight and
sound are distorted, sending
those who consume it far
away from their immediate
environment or even from
themselves.

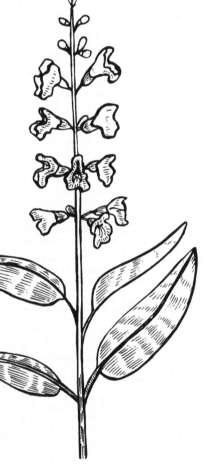

CACAO

Though not really a hallucinogen, cacao is included because of its growing popularity as a ceremonial plant substance. Cacao bean paste is made from pure Criollo or Trinitario beans and brewed into a sort of "hot chocolate." Cacao is a stimulant that can deliver a warm and uplifting "hum" and a sense of elation. In excessive doses, it can induce nausea, sweats, and heart palpitations.

Vision Questing

All shamans know that nature is the greatest teacher. The tradition of leaving the comfort of your ordinary community and entering the arms of the wilderness is ancient and global. There are many kinds of quests for vision, but it is typically seen as a major initiatory event (such as a young man crossing over into manhood). At heart, the core idea is to exit ordinary reality, shed the distractions of safety and comfort, and enter into a dramatic vulnerability to Spirit. Vision quests intend to disassemble seekers from who they have been and reassemble them into the next, bigger form.

Quests may be infused with specific cultural traditions and expectations. For example, it's not uncommon for those on quests to be confined to a small circle for four days and nights without housing, clothing, food, or water. Totally subjecting yourself to the whims of nature, weather, and the spirit of the wilderness, and being truly torn open by deprivation, is essential in disassembling seekers. Some "quests" may include some basic safety like a tent or clothing, while, at the same time, stimulating plenty of fear and vulnerability.

By some thinking, it is the suffering aspect and the exposure of total vulnerability that truly cracks open the hold your ego has on you. The self-imposed severity is a signal to Spirit of your complete and total devotion and commitment. In this thinking, a vision quest without suffering is not really a vision quest at all.

The tradition of "suffering for Spirit" is found throughout religious history. Mortification of the flesh by cutting and whipping, piercing the flesh, crawling on the knees or belly for miles, all as an act of devotion—these practices have been present for millennia in religions such as Hinduism and Christianity, and among many indigenous people such as the Lakota of the Great Plains. A question you may ask yourself is whether extreme suffering inherently creates more spiritual authenticity, or whether it may be a form of institutionalized masochism that humans no longer require, or even whether the drama of the suffering is actually a roundabout act of ego. Is a vision that comes from extreme suffering more authentic than a personally transformative vision that comes with less suffering?

Like every other ecstatic technique, clear intention and preparation are the key to questing. Questing can be very powerful and life threatening, depending on how much suffering you inject into it. If you want to attempt it, know your limits and have someone knowledgeable help you.

Power Animals and Helping Spirits

Without the helping spirits, a shaman is just someone dressed unusually, shaking a rattle. A shaman really should not use the word "me," but rather, "us." Just as the drum, rattle, and other shamanic tools live in both this world and the other world, the shaman is only the visible part of a partnership between the worlds. Shamans see the world as packed full of power that is ready and willing to help them. Trees, plants, mountains, minerals, lakes, and rivers—all kinds of helpers, including animal helpers, are there to lend us their power and wisdom if we listen and ask respectfully.

Years ago, I planned a trip to Laos to meet Hmong tribespeople who live in the hills. At that time, the communist government was still actively killing the Hmong because they had helped the Americans in the Vietnam War. I didn't speak Thai, Lao, or Hmong, nor did I know how to get to the remote Hmong village. I understood that there was plenty of danger, so I hired a guide named Analu. He hired a second guide named Meka to stand guard with a machine gun by the car, as Analu and I hiked across valleys and creeks to get to the village. Both Analu and Meka made specific contributions on our journey. Analu spoke three languages. Meka stood as a sentry.

Just like people bring different skills, every animal in nature has specific powers. Some are strong, others sly, some are vicious, or able to fly or breathe underwater. Power animals protect the shaman from danger, guide them in the other world, advise them how to do things right, and teach them to build their skills and abilities, and, in many cases, it is the spirit guides who do all of the serious work in the other world while the shaman waits to take the results back to the visible world. Shamans know that the animal that appears to them is not an animal, but the embodiment of the spirit of that species. Even more mysteriously, the power animal is the Great Spirit dressed up in his animal "costume" that can shift into other forms over time. Some power animals are temporary; others are lifelong companions.

Traditionally, shamans acquire power animals or guides in a dream, or by asking to meet them in some kind of formalized ceremony or visionary experience. The power animal may be a family totem, or an animal that the shaman has always seemed to have in their life and mind. Sometimes a power animal is one that has attacked the shaman and injured them. Sometimes an elder shaman will ask Spirit to show them the animal guide for someone else, and they will ceremonially "install" that helping spirit into the person.

I have been asked by students why spirit guides would want to help us. The answer is the same as why any of us wants to help anyone else: We have compassion (perhaps because they are in a situation we used to be in), or maybe we are merely intrigued by them, or we feel we have a debt to repay to the world, and this is how we can do it. Perhaps we believe that the way we can serve God, or the Spirit of Love, or our own spiritual evolution, is to help someone else.

Envisioning a Power Animal

The Western world is a shopping culture, and you will end up frustrated if you go shopping for a power animal. The reverse energy is required: Be still, open, receptive, and humble, and ask it to show itself to you. It has already chosen you. It has already been watching you, protecting you, and teaching you in invisible ways. Power animals select the person, not the other way around.

You could use any of the techniques described in this chapter to meet a power animal. Drumming is the most easily effective, and it can be done by asking a friend to drum or rattle for you, or by listening to a recording of shamanic drumming or streaming audio on YouTube.

Begin by creating a receptive and respectful environment around you and inside you. You can make this as ceremonial as you wish—candles, incense, prayers, and singing—or you can just become quiet and open yourself internally.

As the drumming rings out, you can merely clear your mind, or, if you wish, you can imagine yourself in a beautiful natural environment that makes you feel comfortable. Or, you can imagine yourself in a cave, perhaps like the ones ancient people crawled into to paint animal figures on the walls. State your intention clearly, three times—that you wish a power animal to show itself to you and that you are now ready and eager to work with it—because you wish to be of service to the Spirit of Life. This practice of visualizing while the drum plays is called "the shamanic journey to the other world." Be patient and relax.

Allow animal images to appear. When a particularly clear image appears, ask it about its powers and see if you get an answer. Allow more animals to appear if they want to and ask them about their powers. Watch for the one that appears again and again, or the one that feels somehow right. Remember to let IT choose YOU.

If you don't receive a strong sense of an animal showing itself to you, try again at another time. Sometimes the spirits want to make sure you are serious. Ours is a very impatient world, and Spirit sometimes teaches us by not delivering what we want on our time line. If one does appear to you, remember to thank it and praise it. Tell it that it is beautiful, wonderful, or powerful and that you look forward to building a relationship with it. Ask how you can get to know it better and what it wants next from you. Know that you can always decline, or say, "I'm not ready for that yet." Also, remember that a power animal may come to you for a little while, or for a long while. If you have met a power animal, it is good to "feed" it regularly with prayers, praise, thanks, and, if you want, physical offerings like incense, alcohol, water, milk, or something that it tells you it wants. I feed my plant helpers and some animal helpers with song and tobacco smoke. I feed the Crow pieces of meat left at the end of my driveway.

How to Read Power Animals

Please remember the phrase that every shaman understands: "Nature is the best teacher." There are hundreds of books and websites that will tell you what your power animal symbolizes. They can be very helpful, but don't forget that spirits are not symbols—they are living beings just like you. I encourage you to try as much as you can to learn about the animal from their natural behavior.

What is the animal's most obvious strength for survival?

How does it move?

Where does it make its home?

How does it get its food?

How does it defend and protect itself?

How does it get what it wants?

How does it have fun?

How does it relate to others like itself and unlike itself?

How does it relate to humans?

What is most beautiful about it? ("Nothing" is not an acceptable answer!)

What is frightening about it, and why?

How does it communicate? Try to mimic its sound.

What do indigenous cultures say about the animal in their stories?

You can add to the end of each of those questions, "And how could that power (or 'medicine,' or 'wisdom') help me?" Remember that the power animal is really the spirit of that whole species volunteering to work with you. Remember that the word "power" is the important word of "power animal."

AT HOME WITH THE ANIMALS AROUND YOU

Use these simple techniques to connect to the animals surrounding you, seen and unseen, no matter where you live.

- Make a list of animals that you encounter daily in your life.

- Watch for the most obvious ones outside your window. Stand outside your house or apartment and watch the sky and the land.

- Extend the "watch" to the creatures you know are there but don't see. (For example, worms, rats, bats, raccoons, the mycelial network of fungus that is everywhere just beneath the surface of dirt, the fish in the river, or water birds you don't typically see, the insects, even the bacteria and other decomposers.)

- Ask the questions in the **How to Read Power Animals** section (page 56) about each of the animals in your local environment. These are the power animals of your local land. It's okay to work with exotic, dramatic animals not from your landscape, but if you are not in contact with the mythic powers (medicine) of your local fellow creatures, you're not really doing shamanistic work.

- Sometimes a person will meet a mythic or magical creature as a guide, like a dragon or horse with wings. There is certainly nothing wrong with these helpers if they come to you, but they are not strictly "power animals" because power animals should have a life in our ordinary physical realm. Continue to be open to power animals that can also be seen in the physical world, and please don't shortchange the less pretty ones.

SOME COMMON POWER ANIMAL IMAGERY

Cultures vary widely in how they view spirit animals, but here are a few common ones along with some of their associations. Please remember that symbols attached to animals arise from the local land and culture. A heron in Ireland may be seen as quite different from a heron in Minnesota, and from one person to another living on the same land.

HAWK

Hawk flies high, with a wide and sharp vision. It sees more than humans can see. The Cheyenne see the hawk as a protector against enemies and one who brings warnings of danger ahead. The hawk powerfully hunts for what it wants, makes the decision, and goes to get it without doubt stopping it. It helps us refine our skills and make clear decisions without fear. And Hawk reminds me to be sternly ethical.

EAGLE

Like all predators and high-flying birds, Eagle is connected to the wisdom of the upper world and has direct contact with the Creator. Like Hawk, Eagle can deliver solar power—the animating force of all life on earth, and the power of the Divine Masculine—to us, to boost our power, confidence, and integrity.

OWL

Owl is a powerful emissary of night, dark, and death, and is not to be trifled with. In many tribes such as the Navajo, Cherokee, and Kiowa, among many others, the owl is a bad omen, or a bringer of bad news. But because death is full of immense wisdom, Owl is often seen as a carrier of wisdom, insight, and intuition. And because death is one of our larger initiations, Owl is a helper in life's initiations into power. Owl also carries the power of fierce silence, because it is the most silent bird in flight.

CROW

Like all birds, Crow is connected to the upper world, and therefore broad vison. Its dark color connects it to the night, dreaming, death, and great mystery. Crow, like vultures and other carrion eaters, cleans the death force from this world and carries it to the Spirit world for composting. Crows are also trickster spirits who like to have fun. When we befriend the reality of death, life can be more fun and creative, and Crow teaches us not to take ourselves or life too seriously.

WILD CATS

Panther, Lynx, Cougar, Tiger, Lion, and other large wild cats are fierce protector spirits. They have the power of stealth and patience, but when they make a decision, they do not hold back—they don't let doubt interfere. Some are connected more to the night than to the day, and that night vision can help us see through the darkness around us. Large cats can be guides of personal initiation through disassembly or dismemberment of our current identity. The Maya recognize several Jaguar Gods and Goddesses who are associated with diverse skills from fighting to healing.

WATER BIRDS

Water birds move easily between the realms of air, water, and earth. Because they are able to travel easily between the worlds, they help us travel between ordinary and shamanic consciousness, between our world and the Spirit world. Many water birds mate for life and are strong images of devotion and commitment.

HUMMINGBIRD

Hummingbirds are full of quickness and speed. They're often seen as the embodiment of enlightenment—they shimmer with radiance—and the end result of a long, courageous, and transformational spiritual journey. They are also quite fierce and protective.

BUTTERFLY

Almost universally seen as the wondrous spirit of transformation, Butterfly reminds us of just how completely different our shape can become. Its joyful flitting dance, the delicacy of its wings, its utter vulnerability, and its love of life's nectar are the powers of simple joy that comes when we have emerged from the lower self into the higher self.

REINDEER

The Sámi of Northern Scandinavia often see the Reindeer as a mother of life. A story says she sacrificed her heart to be placed at the center of the world so that it would beat life into everything. In the subarctic lands, Reindeer is the only source of food for many months, so she is the generous provider during harsh times, and a reminder to trust Spirit when we are afraid.

DEER

The many kinds of deer that roam the forest are seen as carrying the power of love, gentleness, and total connection to the life force. Most shaman drums are made from deer, and it is said that the deer's core vibration matches very closely with the vibrations of humans. This is why she volunteers herself to help us in so many ways by becoming food, clothing, and tools.

BEAR

Bear is one of the strongest animals, and carries the power of solitude and self-reliance. It is generally gentle and calm in temperament, preferring not to fight meaningless fights, but if threatened, no one will win against it. Bear is a powerful protector and extremely earthy because it regularly reenters the womb of the Mother Earth for long periods of dreaming.

GOAT

The most sure-footed of animals, mountain goats can keep their balance even on the most dangerous of precipices. Goats love to dance, hop, and sing, and they're often seen as spirits who love primal pleasure. When it comes time to fight, however, they charge right at the adversary headfirst with no reserve. Many of the finest musical drums are made from goat skin because it naturally has so many nuanced tones and overtones, further reinforcing their ties to music and dancing.

SNAKE

In cultures as diverse as pre-Christian Europe, ancient Babylon, and the Amazon jungle, the serpent is a feminine symbol of the primal life force and fertility, as well as death, transformation, and resurrection. Its wriggling motion is how all life energy moves: in undulating currents of air, water, thought, and even light. The snake sheds its old skin regularly and is a powerful ally of our rebirth and initiation into a new form.

Conclusion: From Techniques to Tools

It is a wondrous reality that, in many ways, we are not all that different today from the cave painters of 35,000 years ago. We, too, realize that we are swimming among powers greater than us, greater than governments, economies, and technology. We, too, wonder if we can interact with these powers safely, to create more balanced, healthy lives for ourselves. The answer is absolutely yes.

The industrial machine mind will do whatever it can to convince you that you are crazy or making things up or living in a "unicorn fantasy" by pursuing shamanic practice. Modern economies and social structures—what we arrogantly call "the developed world"—depend on the destruction of the ecosystem, and that depends on people believing that there are no powers in nature—only resources to be extracted, and that happiness comes from buying things. Our species is experiencing a great healing and transformation of human consciousness. One way or another, in the next epoch of human history, we will be living with shamanic principles, either through conscious change of consciousness now or through environmental catastrophe.

We've explored the common techniques for "standing outside yourself" and building your relationship with Spirit, and in the next chapter we will explore the tools used by shamans for healing.

Chapter 3

The Shaman's Healing Tools

In this section, we'll explore some of the common cross-cultural tools shamans use today and throughout time. As we'll learn, not every tool is used everywhere— animal skin drums don't play well in extremely humid or wet environments like the Amazon jungle, so rattles are more common. Similarly, in Laos and Korea, a gong is often played in the same way a drum might be played in North America. From the drum to the cap and rattle, prepare to learn about the momentous tools of shamanic healing.

The Shaman's Tools

For modern, industrial-age people, shamanism is often seen as mystical and magical, superstitious, or as just one of many religions. But as we've seen, shamanism is not a religion with a set scripture; it's a spiritual practice.

When it comes to shamanic healing, I see it as exceedingly practical and grounded. In ordinary, visible reality, a plumber has a job, and their tools and clothing help accomplish that job. Owing to their helping spirits and training, shamans see more layers of reality than the Western mind accepts as "real," but the job, as I see it, is similar to more standard work. The plumber sees the clog in the drain and has tools and attire to help remove it. From shoes and coveralls to the "not too wild tie" and white lab coats, we are surrounded by ritual clothing that helps people do their jobs.

Remember that shamanism began not as a theology or prayer practice, but as a practical way to help hunters find the herds, and later as a way to heal. When all is said and done, what matters in shamanic healing is whether it improves someone's life.

Judging success in shamanic healing is complicated, because the shaman is navigating the intersection between the conscious and unconscious minds, between the seen and (usually) unseen layers of reality. It is the shaman's tools that help activate that palpable success.

The Drum

Drums, though they are not the oldest shamanic instrument, are integrally linked to the image of the shaman. Many typical ancient daily tasks of farming, cooking, and building involved repetitive rhythm-making, so it probably didn't take long for humans to begin clicking rocks together or rapping on a hollow log to create the first "shamanic drumming."

There is speculation that wide, shallow drums began as a winnowing tool—probably used by placing wheat or rice into the tray of the drum and tossing it into the air, letting the breeze carry away lighter dirt and chaff, and leaving heavier edible grain to fall back into the drum. The earliest evidence of religious practices most often links the drum with women, and in the diverse religious landscape of pre-Christianity, the drum was a tool of worship for the feminine divine and played exclusively by women.

The drum is the premier tool of shamanism, affirming the drummer's organic connection with all of nature as a divine mother and as a "giving environment," in which all things are imbued with the vibration of Spirit. The drum opens the door to the sacred imagination, to sacred dreaming, and to the world of Spirit found in nature.

For the first Mongolian shamans, the drum was their "spirit horse" that carried them on their journey to the otherworld, as mentioned earlier. For the Siberian Tungus people, the drum was the spirit canoe; for the Evenki, it was the container for all the spirit helpers that the shaman can hold in their hand. This is metaphorical language, but in shamanism, metaphor acknowledges the shape-shifting nature of reality. For the Western mind, a drum cannot also be horse. For the shaman, it certainly can be. Whether you say the drum is your horse or that it entrains brain wave patterns, there is no doubt that the drum changes the consciousness of the drummer and the listener.

The drum itself has layers of symbolism built into it. The vast majority of shamans' drums are round, though some, like the Sámi of Norway, create oval-shaped drums, as do some other Siberian tribes. Some shamans' drums are two-sided, with a skin on each side of the frame. The skin can be made from many kinds of animals, and sometimes fish or other materials. The drums of some Siberian Chuckchee shamans, for example, are made from the dried stomach of a walrus. Some drums, as in Asia, have long handles attached, whereas others do not.

One-sided drums with laced webbing that holds the skin tight onto the frame, or wooden cross bars to hold on to, are common around the world. The roundness is inherently a symbol of the circle of life, time, and the horizon. The laced webbing is symbolically significant, too, as it is not uncommon that it represents the four cardinal directions. The drum itself is sometimes seen as the feminine principle (the "receptive") and the stick as the masculine ("active") principle. Playing the drum unites masculine and feminine energies, which is the base recipe for all life.

All shamans' tools exist partly in this visible world and partly in the otherworld. Whether a shaman buys a drum, has it passed down to them, or makes it with their own hands, the drum must be honored and respected as a wise, living teacher, for it is a guide and a bearer of medicine. The drum is the marriage of life and death. It is also an image of shape-shifting, for the animal, and wood that it is made from, used to be a different shape but now they live and have purpose in the world in an entirely different form. If you have a ritual drum, it's good to "feed" its spirit now and then with incense, tobacco, or words of praise. It is also wise to feed it thanks and praise before beginning any working session with it.

It is common for the shaman's drum to be wrapped up and out of sight except when working. In most traditions, the shaman's drum should be touched only by the shaman.

There are disagreements about whether a drum with a synthetic (plastic) skin is as authentic or powerful as an animal hide drum. These drums are weatherproof and convenient, and often have amazing sound. They change consciousness as well as hide drums. It's for you to decide, but one way to think about a synthetic drum skin is that, since it's made from petroleum, in essence, it is a "dinosaur skin" drum. (Tongue firmly planted in cheek.)

The Rattle

Every shaman's tool can be used for a variety of purposes in healing. The rattle is most commonly used for breaking up blocked or stagnant energy in someone, or cleansing what, in Peru, is called *hucha* (pronounced HOO-chuh)—dense, heavy, or negative energy that clings to the etheric, astral, or mental body. Along with "shaking things loose," the rattle can bring focus and a sense of solidity, and it is also used to direct energy into the body, or wrap a body in protection. Like so much else in shamanic healing practice, it is the *intention*— and what the helping spirits are telling the shaman to do—that matters.

We typically think of a rattle as an orb. As a shamanic tool, it is frequently made of animal skin, gourd, turtle shell, or clay. Inside are the seeds, pebbles, shells, or anything that can make noise. But rattles can also be made of bones tied together, metal pieces, shells tied to a stick or hoop, or even the toenails of goats tied together. In South America, some rattles are made of the dried leaves of the chacapa bush that have been tied together. The sound resembles the wind whooshing through the trees, and it is remarkably hallucinogenic in the hands of a master singer.

The orb of the rattle is a symbol of the Great Mother's womb, which births all new life—and new life is what the healing of the rattle initiates in the patient. Like the drum stick, the rattle handle can be seen as the masculine principle conjoined to the feminine womb. The materials inside carry various powers of nature, including:

Shells carrying ocean power

Stones carrying power from the mineral kingdom

Seeds carrying power of the plant worlds

Feathers used to decorate the rattle carrying the power of the sky world

All of these are present as healing powers in the shaking of the rattle, and any or all can be called in to work on the patient.

A long time ago, I had a dream in which I saw the universe collapsing in on itself and then exploding in the Big Bang. I saw it collapse in again and explode once more, and over and over this process was repeated. Like a camera zooming out, the universe receded into the distance, and then suddenly I was passing through a barrier of some kind. As I continued to zoom out, I realized I had been inside a rattle, shaking in the hand of an old man who was now smiling at me with great glee. "See?!" he said with giddy excitement. The next day, I made my first rattle. While it's hardly a beautiful piece of art, that rattle has quite a bit of mojo, because that old man's glee-ful dream-smile is one of the powers inside it.

Rattles change energy; they shake loose what needs to be shaken loose and assemble anew what needs to be assembled anew. They deconstruct a universe and create it anew.

Crystals (The Mineral Helpers)

Like herds of animals, similar plants, and human communities grouped together, sometimes cultures group portions of nature into realms or nations. Every realm has a special kind of overall power that a shaman may build relationships with, and call upon in healing work. There is the Star nation or Sky realm, a nation of the Sea, and the Animal, Bird, Insect, and Plant nations, too. Every realm has its special kind of power that the shaman may build a relationship with and call upon in healing work.

Minerals can be seen as a nation, too: They are citizens of the inside of the earth, living helpers made from the fire of stars . . . and fed by the water inside the womb of the Great Mother Earth. From the ancient Sumerians to the Greeks and Romans of the Western world, from India and China to the Andes Mountains and New Zealand, healers have called upon the power of crystals, gems, and rocks to aid them in healing.

Crystals are a billion-dollar global business based on their ability to bring specific effects such as psychic protection, cleansing of the body's energy centers, treating depression, bringing peace of mind, or opening "high-frequency" spiritual energies. Crystals are said to be like powerful battery packs that have stored the energy of ancient earth, stars, sun, moon, water, fire, air, and creation itself. They can send that positive energy into the body, as well as extract negative energy from it. Each kind of crystal is described as having its specific "vibration" that interacts with the energy body in different ways to cultivate healing.

Crystals are powerful healers, but they can also be teachers of uncomfortable lessons. Crystals are gorgeous and loaded with mythic energy, but often they come into our hands through a violent process of industrial extraction. This work is frequently done within vulnerable communities in places like the Congo in Africa, and usually as a "side business" of the corporate mining industry. We may not want to think about that when we are meditating in the morning with our crystal, but I consider this to be one of the mineral spirit's best teachings for our time about our relationship to the wider web of life.

One of my first teachers, an initiated shaman in the Mayan tradition, suggested that we consider how much energy the earth put into creating a crystal, and how there was likely no ceremony of asking permission before cracking her open to extract that crystal. If you remember that part of the ancient shaman's job was to do ceremonies that "repay the debt" to the Master of Animals for lives taken, one powerful thing you can do is ask your crystals what kind of ceremony you can perform to repay the debt to the Mother of Crystals for mining them.

Some Popular Healing Crystals and Rocks

Crystals are piezoelectric, which means that when put under pressure (like squeezing or bending) they emit electric energy. The clear quartz crystal is highly piezoelectric and is the backbone of all computer chips. Anything that runs on a computer chip is powered by "crystal energy." Crystals have the ability to store energy and information. Not all beautiful rocks are crystals, but all rocks carry power, each in their own way.

Clear Quartz

Sometimes called the "master healer," this is a very useful mineral to those pursuing shamanic practices. An all-purpose healer, clear quartz works as an amplifier for energy, clarity, and balance. You can ask a nature power, like the sun, to enter the crystal to be held and then direct its energy somewhere. You can also ask clear quartz to draw out negative energy, allowing for a balancing and revitalization of the planes of existence, from physical to emotional to spiritual. Care should be taken to clean any of your crystals periodically or they can amplify the negative energy they have extracted and are holding. Also, know that this crystal can amplify any energy in you and your house, including unconscious anger, envy, or martyrdom. It calls you to be aware of yourself.

Rose Quartz

The color of heart energy and useful in restoring relationships and encouraging harmony, the soft pink rose quartz is a stone of universal love that intrinsically cultivates not only the love of oneself but also friendship and romantic love as well. Hold it on the heart center for healing heartbreak or for opening the power of love or forgiveness. Remember that forgiveness is not easy; it takes great courage and larger vision.

Smoky Quartz

This hazy crystal helps reconnect us to the wonders of being alive by clearing negative energy and restoring emotional balance. For me, it carries the healing power of the night and also speaks to the mystery of suffering and our yearning for clarity and wisdom, as we "see into the glass darkly." Use it to extract or clear confusion, envy, or greed, and to refine your spiritual yearning.

Citrine

A joyful crystal with bright energy that promotes motivation, activates creativity, and enhances concentration. With those citrine-embodied energies present, good fortune, luck, and prosperity can follow. Speak your "manifesting" prayers onto it and ask it to amplify them to the world. Make sure your heart is clear of self-depreciation when you make manifesting prayers.

Amethyst

Amethyst is a protective stone, which at the same time acts as a natural calming agent with healing and cleansing powers. (When you feel protected, you are calmer.) Emotionally, it relieves stress, soothes irritability, and brings sublime joy.

Labradorite

This crystal amplifies psychic energies and spiritual con-
nectedness. It shimmers with light as it moves. Meditation
undertaken with labradorite held in the hands can be more
vivid, and a piece beneath your pillow can inspire colorful,
insightful dreams. Ask it to deliver its powers in measured
doses appropriate to you.

Selenite

A gypsum crystal associated with the cleansing and awakening powers of the moon (Selene is also known as the Greek moon goddess). All the powers of the moon can be held in selenite and worked with: transformation, mothering, lighting the "dark night of the soul" in hard times.

Malachite

A crystal deeply connected to the heart chakra, malachite helps if you are looking for answers in your love life, want to open your heart, or are healing from heartbreak. For me, it has a more ebullient and forceful energy than rose quartz, more like an opera than a lullaby. Also, for me, this stone is more connected to the physical-emotional body than rose quartz, which, for me, tends more toward the mental body.

Fancy Jasper

An opaque quartz known as "the stone of tranquility," fancy jasper helps improve focus and increase concentration. For me, it also has a bit of trickster energy in it, and if you call on it for help, be prepared for help arriving in ways you didn't expect.

Hematite

A renowned "grounding" stone, hematite focuses the heart
and mind on what is tangible, practical, physical, and attain-
able. It reinforces physical and mental strength and can draw
out negative energies. You can ask hematite to extract your
deepest grief (then bury it or wash it in moving water) or to
carry and hold your most tender hope, and connect that hope
into the matrix of your life.

A SIMPLE CLEANSING EXERCISE

This exercise can be done with any kind of crystal or stone you find beautiful or meaningful. Truthfully, you can do this exercise with any rock, because all rocks are our oldest ancestors, carry great wisdom, and contain the energy of the landscape they are from.

Approach the rock, gem, or crystal with a sense of humility and respect, as you would a wise, elder teacher. Ask the stone's permission to work with it. Make sure you feel that permission. The answer may be "not right now," and that is a very good teaching.

Hold it in your hands. Feel its texture, look at it closely, and try to sense its energy. Put aside any question for now of whether you are "making things up" or any sense of embarrassment.

Make a simple prayer of thanks to Mother Earth for this gift of teaching and healing that you are about to receive.

Ask the stone what its healing properties or powers are. Listen for at least three times longer than you think you should.

Ask the stone if it will lend those particular healing powers to you right now, because you have a question, conundrum, or pain that needs cleansing and healing.

Be patient, open, and receptive. Give it plenty of time. Stones are not in a hurry like we are. Let the stone be the boss.

Become aware of anything at all that arises within your thoughts, feelings, or sensations. All of this is teaching and healing, even uncomfortable experiences.

Thank the stone for its help when you feel it is complete.

The Shaman's Cap

Ritual clothing is an important tradition in global shamanism, and as varied as the tribes and landscapes on Earth. Everything is about the shaman's personal symbolism and relationship to their helping spirits. In fact, it is often spirits themselves that dictate exactly how the ritual clothing should be made. Ritual clothing calls a shaman's helping spirits to them, changes the shaman's consciousness, and creates a sense of otherworldliness to onlookers, which can be important for healing to be effective. A headpiece decorated with images of helping spirits or symbols of power acts like a beacon and also a filter, allowing the highest, most beneficial powers to pass in and out of the shaman while blocking negative energy or malevolent spirits.

Across cultures (shamanic and non-shamanic), the head is seen as a gateway to Spirit. The top of the head (crown chakra) and the forehead (third eye) are close to the pineal gland, located in the center of the brain, often called the "seat of the soul." The nape of the neck, which is near the medulla oblongata that joins the brain to the spinal column, is also sometimes seen as a place Spirit enters the body. Like the door to a castle or the front door to your home, the door of the head needs to be open to the right kind of guests and protected from the wrong kind.

The shaman's headpiece can take any form, from a cap made of cloth, fur, hide, or even iron, to an elaborate headpiece that covers much of the upper body. It may be decorated in any way that displays the shaman's personal or cultural cosmology or is meaningful to the people the shaman is working on. In antiquity, the shamans themselves would make their own apparel, something that is less true today in many places. In fact, ritual clothing made by others, with skills, prayers, and intentions, can certainly be powerful. A hat may be simple, or have an explosion of feathers, antlers, bones, or even iron rods attached to it. It may be fringed with feathers, shells, beads, jingles, mirrors, or the fur of specific animals that hang down to cover the shaman's eyes, dancing and swaying as he or she does.

The Shaman's Cloak

Everything previously discussed about a shaman's hat also applies to the shaman's cloak or other ritual clothing. These garments bring the shaman into immediate contact with their spirit guides. At times, these pieces allow the guides to possess the shaman directly. Putting on the costume can be an act of merging with the helping spirits and lending one's body to them.

Siberia reveals the most ancient and dramatic of examples of shamanic garb. There, shamans cloak themselves in the entire hide of a sacred or ritually consecrated animal, including deer, reindeer, elk, or bears. These hides are adorned with shells, beads, bones, and feathers, each one representing a special connection for the shaman. Representations of the sun or moon might also be included on the cloak, or abstract patterns like zigzags that represent power, lightning, the serpent, mountains, or fish teeth. Often small mirrors are hung from the cloak to reflect evil energies back to their source. A more modern example can be found among the Shipibo people of the upper Amazon, whose ritual cloak is called a *cushma*. (*Cush* means "power" in Shipibo.) Cushma are simply constructed, full-length gowns with no attached ornaments. Instead, they have intricately painted or sewn patterns that represent the power of the jungle plants that sing through the shaman as they guide the ceremony all night long.

All of the theatrical elements of ritual—clothing, music, drum, chant, incense, and firelight—create a bubble or island of the *numinous*. The numinous is a timeless, sacred dimension afloat in the profane, mundane, ordinary world. This is another way of saying the shaman opens a doorway to Spirit using the tools of the profession.

Ritual clothing is also important because it protects the shaman from malevolent energies that may be present during the ceremony. Spirits are often attracted to the act of ceremony because a great deal of energy is released between the worlds during these rituals. That energy can be a type of food for spirits. It is for this reason that if you do any kind of ceremony, you want to call protection around you and the space first. Clothing also helps change the consciousness of the people present, allowing them to "suspend disbelief" and enter fully into the sacred drama.

The Shaman's Metaphor (Also Known as Eloquence, Tall Tale, or the Lie)

The shaman's tools we have explored so far have been quite tangible, as you can hold a drum or rattle and touch a cap or cloak. But the shaman also has tools that are less physical.

"Presence" or charisma—the ability to command a space even without speaking—is also important. The singing voice is a critical shaman's tool, and while it doesn't have to be a lovely voice, it needs to carry the confidence, authenticity, sincerity, and power that comes from building a relationship with Spirit over a long, sometimes difficult, study.

A final shaman's tool should also be mentioned here as well: the power to tell a good lie. To wholeheartedly embrace eloquence, poetry, story, and metaphor is a vital piece to shamanic practice. In modern, urban times, we are trained from birth to believe that for something to be true, it must be graspable by the rational mind. If something "doesn't make sense" to our logic center, we say it is not true. If someone insists that it is true, we call them a liar or crazy.

The rational mind is a very good tool, but it has a limited imagination and sense of beauty, and an overdeveloped sense of certainty. In using the metaphor, or the tall tale or lie, the shaman learns to behold many layers of reality simultaneously, and to work with them. There is a common shamanic motto: Nothing is as it appears. And a corollary: Very different things can be true, all at the same time.

And so, as the repetitive beat of a drum or shake of a rattle changes consciousness, as do ritual clothing, candles, incense, and song, so, too, the shaman uses words, images, and story to disarm the rational mind so that Spirit can enter and begin its healing work. The shaman reminds us:

Do not analyze music.

Do not explain dreams.

Do not clarify desire.

The Elusive surrounds all.

The Elusive permeates all.

You must know one thing.

You only need know one thing:

Everything rhymes.

Everything. Rhymes.

Conclusion: The Greater Healing Purpose

I'd like you to remember that owning a shamanic tool doesn't make someone a shaman. The reciprocal relationship with the Spirit of Life, and with the helping spirits of nature, make the shaman, and that is the difficult work. Anyone can buy a horse, but learning to ride is a whole different matter. Much of the Western world is what I call a "shopping culture," and it is very tempting for us to think that the most beautifully made or expensive tool must be the most powerful. That is far from the truth. One of the most beautiful, powerful, and helpful things about the shamanic path is that it just does not operate by the rules of "ordinary" culture.

In this chapter, we've explored a few of the shaman's techniques and tools. We've laid the groundwork for understanding how shamans through time and around the world do their work. Now it is time to explore many pathways for healing the body that are employed by shamans, and how, for the shaman, the body, mind, and spirit are intertwined.

Chapter 4

Healing the Body

What shamans have seen for millennia, physicists have been discovering for 100 years: Reality is composed of many layers beyond the measurable one, and what happens in one layer affects all others. To that end, we'll explore some ways shamans approach healing the body and, in turn, everything else.

While Western medicine focuses on the material body's physical structure and chemical interactions, shamanism acknowledges the "unproven" energetic layers. Consider white willow tree bark, long known by shamans to be useful in pain reduction. Science has "explained" this by discovering salicin, a chemical similar to aspirin, in the bark. Rather than attributing healing to salicin specifically, shamans also see the living spirit of the willow—a feminine, loving, watery spirit—as active in healing the underlying energetic issues that contribute to the body's pain. In a nearly ungraspable way, for both shamans and quantum physicists, there actually is no such thing as the physical world, only certain layers of reality that interact with the five senses of the human.

Body, Mind, and Spirit Intertwined

Shamans are workers with the "unseen." For science, the "unseen" has generally meant "psychological" or "genetic." Shamans have a broader view of what makes up the "unseen" and how it interacts with our visible world and what role it can have on physical health.

Psychology acknowledges how family patterns are handed down through generations. For example, depression and anxiety may be transferred from parent to child to grandchild and onward as learned coping mechanisms or world views.

Shamanism recognizes some passed-down emotional states as "ancestral intrusion." The ancestors have needed healing or attention, and they have asked for it generation after generation, yet their call has not been heard. Korean shamans attribute this to hungry ancestors who project their frustration onto the living. They come from their layer of reality into ours, seeking what they need. Because they are not of this physical layer—they are from a layer with a different vibration—we feel their intrusion in our body as depression or anxiety (or as pain, clumsiness, accidents, or bad luck).

The medical world treats the physical symptoms through physical pharmaceuticals—antidepressants or anti-anxiety medications. Psychotherapy's effectiveness rests on the healing power of the mind, and its approach is centered on rational analysis and the power of mind over behavior.

Shamanism adds to these modalities an understanding that we can actually perform healing on the ancestors in their unseen layer of reality and alleviate their core problems by working within the spirit world. For Western science, to "heal the ancestors" would be an act of traveling backward in time, but for shamans, time is not linear. The ancestors are not in the past, but only in a different layer of present reality. A caveat: Healing the ancestors is particularly challenging, and I advise you not to attempt it without proper training.

Western medicine also acknowledges how emotional trauma can affect physical health. Someone who experiences trauma may be left in a diminished state, listless, or prone to sicknesses of all kinds. Shamans may see the same issue as a need for "realignment of the spirit with the body" or as *soul loss*. When trauma happens, part of our soul, or one of our several souls, may flee the body and become stuck in the spirit world, leaving us with less vital energy, less well-protected psychically, and more prone to accidents, bad luck, and being used by bad people. The shaman's healing approach may be to travel to the spirit world to retrieve the lost soul energy, or to call it back into the body.

The Shaman and Working with Physical Illness

We've already explored how shamanic traditions have a concept of "bad air." The belief is that a spiritual energy has penetrated the person's protective energy field and is now taking up body space or feeding on their vital energy. (As one of my teachers put it: Everything in this world survives by eating something else in this world.) If you live in the Amazon jungle or the African savannah, there are a number of creatures who might see you as food—so you need to be careful. Similar care should be taken to make sure that less physical creatures don't try to dine on your energy.

In shamanic traditions, it may be mere coincidence that you wander by a "hungry spirit" and it begins feeding on you. For some hill tribes in Southeast Asia, you are simply asking for trouble if you wander by a graveyard while whistling a happy tune, since it's a way of making yourself more visible to hungry ghosts. Shamanic traditions also recognize that certain areas of land are dangerous for humans because the spirit of that place feeds on human blood, or a place may want to capture humans and hold them. Hypoxia—fatally losing consciousness at high altitude—is a risk to climbers in some high mountains, and shamans may perceive this as the mountain wanting to keep you with it for its own reasons. Some intersections in cities have far more accidents than average. That may be a traffic management issue, or it may be seen as a "hungry spot." Or that spot may be carrying an insult, and a ceremony conducted for that spot may ease its hunger and reduce accidents.

It may also be that hungry spiritual entities are sent your way by people wishing to do you harm. *Envidia* (or "envy") is a common way that people send spiritual intrusions into others.

In many traditions people can cast "the evil eye" at someone else (or hire a sorcerer to shoot invisible "magic darts"). Even in some isolated Scottish islands today, it is considered rude to look inside a baby carriage and coo with delight about how pretty the baby is. Underlying that perception of "rudeness" is an old belief that to coo over a baby may be a way of trying to eat its pure life energy. Gossip is a mild form of envidia, a way to will ill on people. Shamanism urges us to be careful of the words we use, and to check the actual intent under our speech.

The rational mind can have a difficult time grasping shamanic ideas and perspectives. In many ways, though, Western medicine, psychology, and shamanism are talking about the same things and trying to heal the same issues. Shamanism has its own internal logic, but that logic sees the world through a wide lens. Nearly everyone has experienced being in the presence of someone else who seems to radiate a field of negative energy that affects you even hours later. Many of us have been in a landscape that just doesn't "feel right." And many of us have had relationships with people (parents, friends, lovers) who we can describe as "devouring."

The field of genetics has considered genes to be physical switches that turn on or off. If you are born with one in the wrong position, it destines you to be ill in a certain way. The emerging field of epigenetics describes how genes may be switched on and off by external factors like lifestyle and environment, and how we may be able to switch the genes off or on through gene therapy. The shamanic point of view is that the "external factors" may be in the spirit world, and shamanic healing in the other world may be able to switch genes on and off in this physical world.

There is a long, truly global tradition in shamanism of "the wounded healer." It is a belief that what marks a true shaman is some kind of life-threatening initiatory illness. Like everything else in shamanism, this can be true for some cultures and less important for others where family lineage or dedicated, difficult study is more emphasized. These ideas are made more nuanced by the fact that a mysterious illness 4,000 years ago in Mongolia may be an easily treated sickness today.

When thinking in shamanic terms, a question arises: Over the course of millennia, might the spirits change the way they call shamans into service? I could say that my "shamanic call" came in the form of a tailbone infection that resulted in five days of searing pain and hallucinations until someone dragged me to the doctor for antibiotics. In shamanic tradition, the spirits also call people to service through dreams, or by being recognized by another shaman, or by pure yearning that turns into committed study. Perhaps my call came in the form of a dream where a Lion-Goat-Dog came to rip the top of my head off and breathe pure blue light into me, and I woke up forever different. Or maybe my call was verified when a well-known African shaman met me for the first time, did a divination with seeds and bones, smiled, and said, "It's good to meet a colleague." Regardless, Spirit is capable of calling us into service in any way it wants, and what really matters is the work we do to follow the call.

Hand in Hand with Medicine

Shamanic healing can take many forms, and these healing practices might be viewed on a spectrum from less to more mystical. All shamanic healing practices can be performed in tandem with Western, physical medical practices. Medications, surgery, and psychotherapy all have their effectiveness, and it's not wise to ignore any kind of healing that may be effective. But shamans understand that all physical ailments are accompanied by (or caused by) energetic or spiritual energies. To ignore these less-physical layers is also unwise.

Over time, Western medicine has been steadily opening its preconceptions around shamanic (or energy) healing. For example, it is now becoming fairly common for indigenous healers to partner with Western medical professionals. In

Australia, traditional *ngangkari* healers are on staff at hospitals and clinics to offer ceremonies with protective and cleansing smoke, healing plants, and a type of spiritual massage that moves bad energy out of the body (called "spirit realignment"). In California and Minnesota, Hmong shamans (immigrants from Laos) are routinely invited into hospitals to work alongside doctors to perform ceremonies that keep the patients' souls from running away in fear before surgery, or to protect the body's energy field from the disruption of needles and scalpels. "Doctors are good at disease," the shaman says, "but the soul is the shaman's responsibility." At clinics and hospitals around the Western world, shamanic modalities as well as Reiki, healing touch, and prayer are growing as practices that are "expanding the clinical mind."

The Healing Power of Plants

For shamans, the phrase "medicine is everywhere" is worth repeating like a mantra or prayer. Shamanism emerged from a world in which humans lived by *seeking* and *finding*. For ancient shamans, the earth was a generous mother who gave her gifts of food willingly as long as humans lived in reciprocal gratitude. Seeking and finding certainly included hunting animals, but it also included finding plants for food and healing.

When humans made the turn toward agriculture, they started to become less a wandering creature and more one of settled communities with a more structured daily life. As cities sprang up and then expanded into urban centers defended with heavy walls, an idea began to creep in: inside the city center was civilization, and outside the city walls was dangerous wilderness. Mother Earth transformed from a "giving environment" to a wild thing that needed to be dominated and tamed by man (specifically, men).

The tragedies in this theological turn are voluminous, including the genocide of indigenous people everywhere, and the loss of intimate connection with nature for so many people. An enduring tragedy is that so few people nowadays can wander the land and find the medicine that is everywhere spread out upon the earth.

Plant healers use the physical qualities of plants for physical healing. Plantain, a common lawn weed, has a powerful capacity to stanch bleeding from a wound and remove the itch or sting from insect bites. The leaves of plantain can be chewed and applied as a poultice on the wound. On the energetic level, I have found that plantain can be asked to extract negative energy from our emotional body. Indigenous healers say that the plants that appear on the landscape are the ones needed by the people—that Mother Earth is sending the medicine we need. Do our lawns have so much plantain in them because we have so much negative energy that needs healing?

The use of "plant baths" blends the physical and less physical aspect of plants' healing powers. Several plants with various healing qualities are put into a basin or tub to steep in water and, when ready, the water with the plants is poured over the patient. The patient may also immerse themselves into the bath or use the steam from the bath to cleanse their energy body. The physical body absorbs the physical healing qualities of the plants and the energy body also takes in the spiritual energies of the plants.

Traditional plant healers learn the physical properties of plants in healing, but they also come into deep relationship with the spirit of the plant and may be taught how the plant can heal in more esoteric ways. A South American *vegetelista* may tell you that they receive their healing abilities directly from the *genios,* the mother spirit of the plant species, and from the *arkana,* which are the protective spirits of the plants. In the Celtic world, healers are routinely taught how to use plants by the faeries. Wherever you go in the animistic world, the plant doctors affirm that the spirits of plants teach them what they need to know.

SOME HEALING PLANTS AND THEIR USES

Plants have powerful physical properties that can heal the body, but they also have living spirits that are called in to heal the non-visible parts of the body.

CEDAR

Among North American tribes, cedar smoke is used to purify the home and also used in ceremonies for protection, as it is said to chase away bad spirits. Cedar can also be made into a tea. For me, cedar can be called on to remind us of the joy present in our lives.

MARIGOLD

A natural antiseptic from as far back as ancient Europe, the marigold (also called calendula) is useful in topical application. Wounds, burns, rashes, insect bites, and mild swelling can all be treated with marigold, as it is both an anti-inflammatory and an antioxidant. The Central American marigold species *Tagetes lucida* is used ceremonially as an offering for the dead, a repellant of evil, and a sedative and aphrodisiac if smoked. For me, marigold also reminds us that it is perfectly okay—and perhaps even part of our sacred duty—to be a happy person even in an anxious and fearful world.

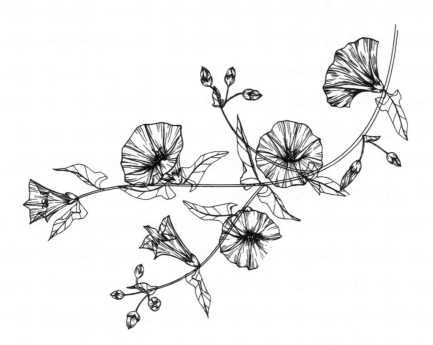

MORNING GLORY

Often found in gardens in North America, morning glory (*Ipomoea violacea*) is a vine with many varieties and hues of flowers. Native Mexican tribes long ago discovered that morning glory seeds that are eaten or ground up and soaked in water can yield potent psychoactive results. Specific varieties of psycho-active morning glories—all cleverly named—include: Heavenly Blue, Summer Skies, Flying Saucers, Wedding Bells, and Pearly Gates.

MUGWORT

A ritual incense in the Aztec tradition, mugwort honors the goddess of salt and salt miners. Mugwort is also common in Europe, as Nordic tradition explains that it was one of the nine sacred herbs that Odin gifted to the world. Mugwort has been used for centuries for a great number of things, from the psychedelic (inducing astral projection and lucid dreaming) to the practical (repelling insects from gardens).

TOBACCO

The powerful rainforest tobacco *Nicotiana rustica* is used in healing ceremonies to drive away bad energies, purify a space, call in protection, or carry the intention or prayer of the healer. Smoke is blown across or around the body, or the plant itself is smoked by the patient.

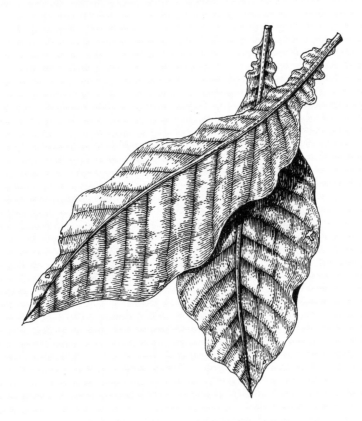

SAGE

Similar to mugwort, sage has uses that are both mundane and profound. For the people of the American plains, white prairie sage (*Artemisia ludoviciana*) is a significant tool in cultivating health, as it is both innately antimicrobial and antibacterial. Both white prairie sage and white sage (*Salvia apiana*) are effective at repelling insects. Ceremonially used, sage can be burned for purifying space or clearing negative spiritual energies. Some believe that only *Salvia apiana*, a variety native to the southwestern United States and northwestern Mexico, suitable for such cleansing uses.

SWEET GRASS

The aroma of sweet grass instills gentleness into the space or the hearts of people. "The sacred hair of Mother Earth" to native North Americans, sweet grass is often woven into a three-strand braid. Together, the strands represent love, kindness, and honesty. Additionally, sweet grass is a useful plant in purification ceremonies.

USNEA

A lichen that thrives on trees, usnea is a versatile and useful tool when treating pain and discomfort. Medicine people of the American great plains have used this moss not only to break fevers and heal wounds, but also to relieve pain, induce weight loss, and clear phlegm from the lungs. When gargled or swallowed, usnea is useful in relieving soreness in the mouth or throat.

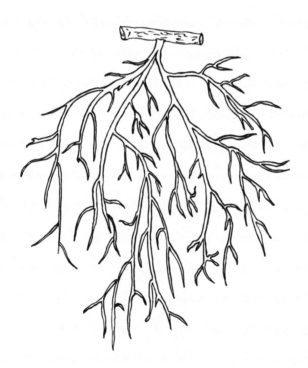

The Healing Touch of Massage

Sometimes your body develops "knots" in the muscles. We all have experienced this. Whether because of stress, overactivity or inactivity, diet, repetitive motion, or injury, knots are painful lumps that can actually be felt with the fingers. Pressing on or rubbing them (a form of physical deep tissue massage) is often the way to release and "clear" the stored tension in the muscle and get it to open and relax. Similar "knots" in the energy body also exist and can be opened, cleared, and healed.

Shamans understand that the human body has many layers to it, but most are unseen. The physical body can be called the densest or most compact layer, and it can be felt with the fingers. But there are several less physical, more energetic layers surrounding the physical body, and they cannot be felt by the physical hands or seen with the eyes. These layers "vibrate" differently than the physical body does.

Shamans see all of reality as vibration. Everything vibrates at its own frequency. A mountain has a different frequency than a lake or a deer or a dragonfly. A shaman's way of saying this might be, "Every creature sings its own unique song in the great symphony of the universe." Celtic shamans call the universe the "Great Song" (*Oran Mor*), and each creature has its own small song that comes from its heart (*Oran Cridhe*, with the second word pronounced kree).

Some spiritual traditions teach that that there are five distinct layers to the body, including the physical layer. Some teach there are thirteen layers. The physical body vibrates at the lowest frequency, and each energetic layer vibrates at successively higher frequencies. The non-physical layers of the body are called by several names, including the energy body, auric field, spiritual body, "bubble," or "luminous body" (what in Andean tradition is called the *kausay poq'po*). Healing can be done on any of these layers of the body.

As the body can store energy in the form of a knotted muscle, it can also store psychic or emotional energy that may or may not show up palpably in the physical body. The causes of energetic "knots" are similar to physical ones: being under constant or repetitive emotional stress, having a need to constantly defend your psychic self from attack, being wounded psychically, or simply not clearing regular negative energy that you pick up as an ordinary part of life, much as shoes pick up dirt.

Your energy body can also store all sorts of intrusions, like the cursing energy sent your way by others (*envidia*) or "magic darts" mentioned earlier. Many shamanic traditions use physical massage to clear away non-physical energies. By rubbing the body, the healer may also be manipulating the energy body to release stored energies. That "energy massage" can also be done with singing, or by using smoke, plants, or prayer.

One way you can apply these ideas in your own life is to work with a massage therapist who understands the connection between the knotted muscle and stored energy. As the therapist is working on the physical knot, you can be in a state of prayer, asking Spirit or your helping spirits (whether or not you are keenly aware) to simultaneously clear any energetic intrusions or knots. At the end of the day, you can also do a simple meditation, prayer, or visualization that asks your helping spirits to clear away any negative energy that has clung to you during the day. These spirits may take it down into the earth where it is happily composted by the Earth Mother.

The Healing of Emotional Release

Like a knot in a muscle or an intrusion in the energy body, emotions often become "knotted." In shamanic terms, this is when our emotional body falls ill. There are many cultural messages encouraging us to repress our emotions or dress up a truer one with a different emotion.

For example, oftentimes anger is actually grieving or fear dressed up in a more acceptable form. Instead of grieving a loss, we transmute that grief into blame and then express it as anger. Much of the increase in random anger, from road rage to social media–driven angst, is about the fact that we are not allowed to honestly express grief. However, expressing grief as anger is quite acceptable. We fall into trouble here because expressing an emotion dressed up in a false costume means that the true emotion doesn't actually get expressed. When repressed, that feeling sinks into the emotional body and becomes a "knot" of energy that will begin to affect mental and physical health at some point.

A teacher of mine once said America is a fire and air culture that has fallen terribly out of balance with the elements of water and earth. Fiery energies are viewed as a sign of masculine strength, and long, dry, "airy" intellectualizing is seen as brilliance. Watery energies like grief, love, and compassion, and the earthy energies of silence or simplicity, are viewed as feminine, and therefore weak. This is one of the core illnesses of Western culture.

One basic healing act you can do is to become aware of the true emotion you are feeling at any given moment and express it clearly. When you feel an emotion, ask yourself if there is really another, less acceptable emotion hiding underneath it. To help sort out the true from the disguised, it may help to explore some of the emotive types.

Negative emotions generally fit into five distinct categories.

Anger: Thoughts that center around being treated unfairly or having been done wrong or harmed, "should" thoughts, and thoughts of rules being circumvented or broken altogether

Anxiety: "What-ifs" that run amok, concerns that bad things are going to happen in the future, and thoughts about danger, threats, or risk

Embarrassment: Thoughts about the concerns of others, and worry about unfair judgment of flaws or mistakes

Guilt: Thoughts of previous ills committed against someone else, thoughts of failing to live up to your own moral standards, and a misplaced sense of regret or responsibility for negative outcomes

Sadness: Thoughts that are critical of the self, pessimism, and thoughts of loss or failure

Understanding what kind of power is wracking you is useful in cultivating a good healing practice. Oftentimes when I say or believe that I'm feeling anxious, the reality is that I'm not. I'm angry. However, I know that admitting to being angry is less palatable than being anxious. I don't like to think of myself as an angry person, so I will mask my true feeling with one that is viewed as more acceptable. This can happen regularly, as it's not uncommon for true emotions to hide underneath another, more easily broadcast one. While it might feel like you're feeling all of your emotions simultaneously, it's useful to dig deeper and investigate what the root emotion is. Once you reach it, feel this base emotion truthfully, without judgment.

This is far more difficult than it may sound. Begin with allowing yourself to grieve fully. One powerful practice you can do is to lie on the earth and ask the Great Mother to take your tears. This can be an immensely cleansing healing practice.

Healing with Heat

Throughout history, humans have used enclosed spaces filled with heat or steam to cleanse the body and spirit, most often as a communal experience. The earliest bath found dates to 4,500 years ago in Pakistan. From Turkish baths (*hammans*), Russian *banyas*, Roman baths, Japanese *onsens*, and Korean *jimjilbangs,* to Finnish saunas and Native American sweat lodges, baths and steam houses are found everywhere. Some of these houses of heat are more directly ceremonial than others, but all of them certainly provide healing of the body's many energetic layers and repair spiritual wounds, primarily through the purging (sweating out) of stored energy or toxins, and cleansing of the skin.

Whether the spiritual element is overt or not, the house of heat is packed with wonderful spiritual imagery. The structure itself—whether it is built of bent branches like a sweat lodge, wood like a Finnish sauna, or even cut out of a hill—can be seen as the womb of the Earth Mother. When we enter it, we are entering her revivifying embrace. In most heat houses, the heat radiates from rocks that have been heated in the fire. This can be seen as asking the elements of earth (rocks) and fire for help with healing. If water is poured over the hot rocks for steam, this is asking the elements water and air to help heal us. If dried herbs or fragrant tinctures are put on the hot rocks, this is asking the plant realm to help us. For the sweat lodge, animal hides can be used to cover the bent branches, and this is asking the animal realm to help us. The altered state that can be summoned by the steam is a way of opening ourselves and connecting to our spirit helpers. The house of heat opens the doors between the two worlds, and we can make prayers for our unseen and seen relatives alike.

There are some ways you can bring healing with heat into your life. Certainly, you can build a sauna in your house or yard, but I urge you not to build a sweat lodge unless you have been thoroughly trained in the tradition by Native elders and they have given you explicit permission. Sweat lodges, and any house of heat, can be dangerous, especially if you approach them with arrogance, ignorance, or disrespect. However, even if you use the sauna at the place you exercise, you can enter it with a sacred mindset and honor all the same powers of earth, fire, water, and air to help cleanse and heal you. Even when you have a stuffy nose and you breathe steam from a pot with a towel over your head, you can still ask the spirits involved for help, and thank them. There's never a wrong time to praise the spirits of nature for their gifts of healing.

Healing with the Hands

We know, because we can feel it, that we can transfer energy with a gaze—love, desire, sympathy, anger, or even curses are examples of this. Hands also transmit energy and are marvelous healing tools. We can bring calm and confidence to someone merely by placing a hand on their shoulder. We can be trained to increase the flow of energy from our hands and increase their effectiveness in turn as healing tools.

The hands have energy centers (chakras) in the palms, and in each of the finger joints. By learning to work with the energy centers, we can transmit or receive energy from others. Much of the healing modality of Reiki is centered in this. Some traditions say that the left hand is a receiver of energy and the right hand a transmitter. Others say that your dominant hand is the transmitter, and your non-dominant hand the receiver.

To work with the hands, try rubbing them together for a few moments to create warmth. At the same time, put intention into them to clear out any negative energy that you are carrying, making your hands a "clear channel."

Hold your hands a few inches apart and feel or try to see (with the spiritual eye) a ball of energy floating between them. Look at the palms and sense, or "see," the energy in the palms. Ask Spirit, or your helping spirits, to fill that energy with healing love, or pure healing light.

A more shamanic approach to this is to ask a spirit of nature—a tree, the sun, the moon, a mountain, or a river—to fill your hands with healing power. When you are ready, you can place them on yourself or on someone else.

I recommend you focus on sending love energy into someone, but unless you get training, don't draw energy out of them, and do not do any of this without the person's expressed permission.

When you are finished, clean your hands by blowing on them, asking Spirit to clear off any energy you have collected from the person, wash them in warm or salt water, or pass them over the flame of a candle or through sage smoke.

THE DIFFERENCE BETWEEN HEALING AND CURING

In Western medicine, pain can be "cured" with drugs, and disease can be cured with medical treatment. Surgery could be a cure for a bad knee or a blocked heart artery. None of that means you won't die someday—you will. Life is incurable. You will also suffer again in some way, because life in the human body includes suffering—it's the nature of this particular universe.

Curing is about the dense flesh, the lowest vibrating layer of the human body. When we are in pain or in fear of dying, curing can, understandably, become our sole focus. But healing is about restoring the balance between the many layers of the body, and between the soul and the body. Shamans understand that imbalances among the unseen energetic layers of the body show up as physical symptoms. Simply taking pain away from the flesh may be curing the flesh layer but not healing the whole body.

Both curing and healing are about how suffering shrinks us into a smaller shape than we are meant to be; how suffering makes us hard-hearted, distracted, mean, or unable to think of anything but our own suffering. Healing is about our response to the reality of suffering and our relationship to all of life.

Someone can be cured of a disease but remain mired in self-centered martyrdom, anger, and bitterness. Sometimes curing the pain will also open the person's heart, and they will go on to live in a different, more expansive way. That's healing. And, in one of the greatest mysteries of being human, sometimes a person's disease is not curable, the pain is not totally controllable, and yet, their heart, imagination, and sense of their true identity as Spirit-in-flesh can be awakened. Their compassion, curiosity, and wonder can even expand as they realize death is coming sooner than they had hoped. This is healing.

Conclusion

Shamans understand the poet Walt Whitman's words: "I am large; I contain multitudes." Life is bigger, deeper, more nuanced, and more magnificent than we can see with our physical eyes. As we've seen, the body is made of layers of energy, and shamans understand the world as a vast interplay of living energies, many of them not discernible by the five senses.

We live in a world where the Spirit of Life (or the Creator) dresses itself up joyfully in infinite costumes, whether as plants, animals, minerals, elements, or human beings. The life force that animates every creature flows in multiple layers of vibration through everything. Healing can be (or must be) applied to all layers for it to truly be called healing. In the next chapter, we will explore some of the layers of the universe and how you can use ancient shamanic techniques for accessing them for personal healing.

Chapter 5

The Healing
Spiritual Journey

In the previous chapter, we discussed
how shamans understand that the densest
levels of reality are the ones discernible
by the five senses. Devices like
microscopes, telescopes, sonar, and
radar amplify our five senses but are
still looking at the most dense level of
reality. In this chapter, we will explore
how shamans learn to perceive other,
non-physical, layers of reality.

The Shaman's States of Consciousness

Every kind of creature has its particular set of skills and powers. Gazelles can run fast and leap high, squirrels have incredible balance, hawks possess powerful eyes that can see far, and crabs manipulate massive claws. Humans, too, contain inborn skills that make them human. We have a powerfully rational mind and opposable thumbs that, together, allow us to design and build things. Also, to be human is to have the innate ability to change consciousness, to travel between the worlds.

Every human being has an "ordinary consciousness" used to navigate our daily tasks of our contemporary society and the physical realm. But we also each have access to what may be called a "shamanic consciousness"—the "higher mind" with which we come into contact with larger awareness. For most of us, that larger awareness appears in brief peak experiences where we feel awash in wonder and connected to all of life in a dramatic way. In such moments, we may be overwhelmed by love, awe, and gratitude and feel deeply at peace. We may spend a lifetime trying to re-create that temporary experience.

The ordinary state of consciousness is based in the physical body and is therefore deeply influenced by many fears: of death, entrapment, abandonment, of being all alone in the universe, and of meaninglessness. Those fears manifest themselves as personality traits such as arrogance, self-deprecation, impatience, blame, greed, envy, and stubbornness. This is the small, lower, or false self—the ego—that every spiritual path acknowledges is part of being human.

The other consciousness is influenced by our higher, larger, or true self—our soul or Essence, which is always connected to "Source," Spirit, or the Creator. Most often, this part of us speaks in whispers while the lower self is shouting, cursing, complaining, and blaming. At times, the higher self will sweep us out of the lower self and into one of the temporary peak experiences.

The denser, physical levels tend to be run more by fear and desire, both of which have a narrow vision and need for control. The higher vibrational, less dense, less physical levels of reality tend to operate from a place of love and wisdom and possess expansive vision and openness. Shamanic practice is about learning to access more layers and states of consciousness, to free oneself from the bondage of fear and desire (at least temporarily) and draw the powers of the higher vibration layers into the lower levels to deliver transformative healing.

When the shaman of the Arctic journeys to the Reindeer Spirit to ask for information about a patient, that spirit does not exist in the shaman's mind—it is not a figment of the imagination. It exists in a real, non-visible world that can be accessed only through opening a door to a different consciousness. The Reindeer is not the physical reindeer, but the high-vibration "spirit" of the species, and it is not bound by physical laws. The Reindeer Spirit can fly, speak, sing, dive into the ocean, dance, and shape-shift. When the shaman journeys to the spirit of a plant to be taught a healing song, that song, taught in the spirit world and carried back through the doorway, will bring physical healing when sung into the body in the physical world. When the shaman is taken by beings of light to have their flesh removed and bathed in a crystalline pool, that is not a daydream, but a visit to a foreign land and healing in that place.

The World Tree and the Three Realms

Humans understand that we cannot fly and we cannot live underwater or inside the deep earth. Instead, we live on the earth's surface, in between the two "beyonds"—the above and the below—that hold mysterious power for us. For humans around the world, trees have long been a symbol for this structure of the universe.

The tree's leafy branches reach into the celestial realm of the "upper world" and draw down the powers of light and fire from the sun, stars, and moon, as well as the freedom of the birds and the ephemerality of the ever-shifting winds. The tree's roots reach into "lower world" and draw up the powers of the dark earth and deep waters, the ancestors, sea creatures, minerals, and the life force in the plants. Here in the "middle world," where humans live, the upper and lower worlds marry in the trunk of the tree.

The Tree of Life is also inside us. Our head is the realm of thinking, the place where the Great Immensity, the Divine Masculine, sings its prophetic songs and speaks its new ideas down into us. Our belly is the realm of physical power and will, the place where the Divine Feminine sings its song of survival, beauty, and pleasure up into us. Our arms are the upward-reaching branches, and our legs are the downward-yearning roots.

The human heart is where the above and below marry inside us. The human body is the Tree of Life: a marriage of the Divine Masculine and the Divine Feminine, of fire, air, earth, and water. We are the marriage of wisdom, power, and love. We also understand that wherever we are, we are surrounded by the six directions (east, south, west, north, up,

THE WORLD TREE
(THE TREE OF LIFE)

The Upper World

The Middle World

The Lower World

and down). The seventh direction is our heart, the center of our body, where all the spiritual directions meet and marry.

Shamans can journey to the non-physical layers of each realm—the below, above, and middle as well as each of the seven directions—for information and healing. Each of the three worlds and each of the seven directions has its own healing powers for the shaman to access. The shaman may choose which realm they will journey to, or the helping spirits will make the choice based on the question or problem the shaman is trying to solve. There are many ways to enter the three realms and work with them, as we will now explore.

A TREE OF LIFE MEDITATION

This meditation will help you enter into the expansive state of consciousness that connects you to both the great above and deep below. Rooted in the concept of the Tree of Life, this meditation can be as brief as a few minutes or take far longer (even better).

To begin, find a comfortable position for your body, whether sitting, lying down, or standing.

Relax, and take a few deep breaths with your eyes closed.

Breathe in deeply through the nose, and blow out forcefully through the mouth as a way of expelling stored negative energy in the body. Expel as much breath as you can. Take at least seven of these breaths.

Imagine yourself as a large tree. See yourself reaching upward, splitting into four large branches, each going off into the cardinal directions (east, south, west, and north). See your leaves facing upward toward the sun. As you imagine, place your attention on your body, and let physical sensations arise if they want to. A sense of warmth, tingling, "energy," or even emotions can be part of the experience.

Imagine you have four large roots, plunging down into the earth, each leading away into the cardinal directions, and one central tap root heading straight down into the center of the earth.

Feel the sunshine falling on the leaves and being taken down through the branches and into the trunk. Feel the roots drawing the power of earth and water upward into the trunk.

Feel the energy of the above world—the divine masculine energy of infinity—flowing down into your head, down into the heart and the belly, and then circulating all through your body. Let this take some time.

Feel the energy of the below world—the divine feminine energy of earth—flowing up through your feet, legs, pelvis, belly, and heart, and into the head, circulating all through your body. Let this take some time.

Feel the two energies, the above and the below, meet in your heart. Feel them swirl together in a dance of delight, love, and respect. Let that marriage of energies flow through your entire body. You may feel energy, warmth, light, color, vibration, or emotion as you do this.

Recognize that your body *is* the tree of life! When you are finished, give thanks to Spirit for making you like this.

The Importance of Trance

In order to work in a healing way, shamans enter a trance state—a non-ordinary state of wakefulness in which they are no longer self-aware, and outside stimuli does not affect them. The trance widens the shaman's vision, releases them to some extent from their lower self, and allows them to see deeper, more ethereal layers of reality.

Humans actually move into trance quite easily, whether the body is active or inactive. All daydreaming is trance, as is being "lost" in thought. Intense concentration is a kind of trance, like reading a book, watching TV, playing video games, or painting a picture. As we touched on in chapter 2, any repetitive rhythm can bring on a trance state (drumming, rattling, and dancing). On the physical spectrum, meditation, prayer, exercise, and lovemaking can all create a kind of trance. Even less enjoyable situations like sustained grief, physical pain, or worry can do so.

Anytime you "step out of your ordinary mind," or lose a sense of being observed by the world or by yourself, you have fallen into a trance. In a trance state, you step away from your ego, from the "I" that is always judging its immediate surroundings and your place in them. The ego's job is to keep you safe from harm, so it is always looking for the physical danger of being hurt or killed and the social danger of being embarrassed or humiliated.

In order to do shamanic work, one must step outside the rules that the bodyguard of the ego sets for us. Shamanic teachers call this "getting out of your own way" or "making yourself a hollow bone." This refers to the ancient bone flute, maybe the first musical instrument crafted by humans. Just as a flute must be completely free of any obstructions so that air passes through and makes music, the constant stream of judgment (of others and of self) that the ego engages in must be equally quelled in order for Spirit to use the shaman as its instrument.

Most trance is quite light and used merely to relax and shut off the whirlwind of thought. In shamanic practice, a deeper trance is needed to open the door to Spirit, to work between the worlds with the helping spirits. Most commonly, the shaman's trance is achieved and induced by drumming or rattling, which opens the shaman's vision so they can see spirit guides or the patient's energy field. Heavier trances may be needed to travel to the lower, middle, or upper world, and yet the shaman may still be able to speak to people in this physical world. The use of entheogens induces the heaviest trance, which effectively removes the shaman's presence from this world for a while.

Brain research shows that, in the shaman's trance, the source of information coming from the brain shifts from the usually dominant, rational left brain to the experiential, metaphorical, and poetic right brain. In short, the shaman moves into the in-between place—the place between worlds, the threshold between waking and dreaming—where the door to Spirit opens, where everything has more than one "meaning," and where "everything rhymes."

Traveling to the Three Worlds

Shamans can travel to any of the three worlds, depending on the issue they are trying to resolve or receive guidance on. In this section, I'll describe the journeys to the lower and upper worlds first and then focus on the middle world.

It is not possible to definitively state which qualities are present in which world—similar qualities can be seen in all the worlds, and often all of it is culturally conditioned or personal to each shaman. One shaman may journey to the lower world to ask the ancestors for help; another may seek the ancestors in the upper world. In any of the three worlds, the shaman may encounter animal guides or spirits that take human shape, or they may see structures or natural landscapes.

However, there does seem to be some generalized "feeling" for each world that shamans may agree upon. The lower world has a somewhat denser, thicker, or heavier feel to it than the upper world, which can feel airy. The lower world also tends to be more populated with plants, trees, forests, jungles, and animals than the upper world, which often feels more spacious. The lower world may have more vibrant colors and more structures like huts or villages as well.

Healing by Descending to the Lower World

Shamans may travel to the lower world in many ways, but usually they do so by finding an opening into the ground. A shaman may enter a tree root and follow it down (perhaps a root of the Tree of Life, as described previously). A shaman may follow a tunnel into the earth, enter a cave passageway that heads downward, descend into a well, or follow flowing water that enters the earth somehow. They are not journeying into the *ground*, though—not into dirt and gravel—but into an alternate layer of reality that is accessed first by seeming to travel downward *through* the physical earth, then passing through a barrier into a new layer of reality.

If there is a core quality of the lower world, perhaps it is "primal life power." Journeys to the lower world are most often for gathering some type of functional, practical power to be used in the human world. The lower world journey is most often about asking for the diagnosis and treatment of an illness or suffering in the human world. Sometimes the treatment for the illness happens in the lower world, like performing a kind of energetic surgery on the patient's spirit body. Other times, the treatment delivered by the spirits in the lower world is meant to be conducted in the ordinary world, like a public ceremony, a potion made of plant medicines, a plant bath, or an energy massage.

There are essentially three kinds of illnesses, and a lower world journey can help address any of them. They are:

Physical illness (disease, pain, injury)

Emotional or mental illness (depression, anxiety, grief)

Communal illness (discord between individuals, family, or nations, or between people and nature)

In a lower world journey, the shaman may find that a depressed person needs to have a piece of their missing soul returned to their body, that a physical illness is the result of a spiritual intrusion, or that an injury was the result of an insult made to a nature spirit or because of an unhealed ancestor.

The shaman may perform the healing in the spirit world— for instance, finding a lost soul part, bringing it back, and blowing it into the patient's body. In the case of the insulted nature spirit, the shaman may resolve the insult by talking with the spirit in the lower world, or they may discover that the treatment requires the patient to make offerings of flowers, food, tobacco, alcohol, milk, or incense to that spirit in the ordinary world, perhaps in the very location where the insult occurred.

One way to think about the power of the lower world is this: The soil is the place of food, growth, sex, the body, death, physical transformation, healing plants, intimacy, and immediacy. Journeys to the lower world often carry these themes. An example in literature of a lower world journey is *Alice in Wonderland*. Thematically, the story is an initiation into adulthood (or, mythically, the "next higher state of being") through a lower world journey. She follows the rabbit (a power animal) down the hole into an alternate world where she meets a series of animal and human teachers. Likewise, the Greek tale of Hercules's descent into Hades to accomplish initiatory tasks is also a lower world journey, as are Celtic tales of the hero being taken down into the green faerie mounds for unending dancing, feasting, and fornicating.

Healing by Ascending to the Upper World

The upper world journey is most often accessed by passing through some kind of hole in the sky. Sometimes the North Star is the doorway, or the Big Dipper. Sometimes, the shaman climbs up the Tree of Life. In many ancient cultures, there was a central fire in the yurt, hut, or tipi, and shamans could access the upper world by riding the smoke up and out of the smoke hole.

For modern practitioners of shamanism, lower world journeys routinely seem easier to accomplish than upper world journeys, which are often fraught with resistance or frustration. The lower world seems rather quickly accessed through the tunnel or root, whereas the upper world may require a more complex, multi-stage journey. For example, crossing a vast range of mountains, then riding a bird to the top of a peak, then calling out for a rope to drop and climbing up. One explanation is that the lower world is vibrationally closer to the middle world where we live, whereas the upper world vibrates at a higher frequency. The lower world seems generally more physical and emotional, and the upper world can be more mental. This does not mean the upper world is smarter or wiser. It is just a different "song."

A shaman may go to the upper world for the same reason they go to the lower world, but they may be personally or culturally attuned to one realm over the other. Or, it may be that their helping spirits decide that, for this particular patient or issue, this is the particular realm from which to seek help.

In general, as the lower world is accessed for primal life power, often for healing and for a first meeting with a power animal, the upper world is accessed for expansive wisdom, for answers to existential questions, or for greater vision and spiritual understanding.

The sky is the place of spaciousness and expansiveness, of eternity, infinity, and larger vision. So, it would be a little more common for a shaman to access the lower world to heal an individual body and access the upper world to ask for healing or guidance for the whole tribe. Again, these are generalizations that can break down quite easily.

In literature, *The Wizard of Oz* is an initiatory tale involving an upper world journey. Dorothy is swept up by the tornado and taken to a gleaming city watched over by a wise wizard. There is a great deal of flying in the story. The themes are less body-oriented and more philosophical. *Jack and the Beanstalk* is a tale of a journey to the upper world. The Harry Potter stories are packed full of both lower and upper world shamanic themes.

Healing within the Middle World

A middle world journey takes the shaman into the hidden parts of the "real" world, or into the spiritual aspects of nature. A shaman may journey to a faraway location in the real world, or to a different time in the real world.

The classic middle world journey might be to locate the herd for hunting. A shaman may become a bird and fly high, searching the landscape for the herd. Or the shaman may shape-shift into a bird or animal to spy on another tribe of people. A shaman from that tribe may very well be able to spot the shape-shifted shaman. A common middle world journey involves the shaman finding lost objects or people, or "checking in" on someone who is far away.

The distinction between middle and lower world journeys can be blurry. A shaman may meet the spirit of a plant or animal species, or an elemental spirit of water or fire in a middle world or a lower world journey. (And they may meet the "upper world aspect" of that spirit in the upper world journey.) The distinction really is whether or not the shaman uses the descending portal or entrance in the lower world journey, or whether they travel more "horizontally" into the hidden energies of nature (middle world).

Each plant and animal possesses a guiding spirit, sometimes called the Mother of that creature. Often, natural areas of land, like a stretch of forest, have a guardian spirit who protects the many plants and creatures of that area. When a shaman journeys to meet or speak to these local nature spirits, it is a middle world journey. In healing, when a shaman opens their vision to see the patient's energy body and work on it, this is healing in the Middle World. "Remote" healing—where a healer is a long distance from the patient—is a way of working in the middle world.

European faerie tales are chock-full of middle world journeys. A common theme is the Celtic hero who gives chase to a radiant animal (often a white deer) or lovely woman, but cannot seem to catch them no matter how fast he rides. A sudden mist arises, and, as he rides through it, he emerges into the Celtic spirit world. He often ends up meeting a radiantly dressed figure who offers wisdom or power. Chance meetings with faeries, gnomes, leprechauns, sprites, and other mythic forest creatures are typically middle world journeys. Tales of magical sea voyages like *Sinbad* and the classic Greek tale *The Odyssey* are also middle world journeys, as is *The Lion, the Witch and the Wardrobe*. Each could also be seen as a lower world journey, so again, the boundaries are not solid.

Evil in the Three Worlds

Evil is a mammoth topic beyond the scope of this book, but in general, malevolent spirits are more populous in the middle world than in the other two realms. This may be because the middle world is just outside the boundary of the physical world and they blend easily. It is also the place where people who have died can become trapped with regret, anger, or shame. Many nature spirits are tricksters or chaotic in nature, and we can mistake that as evil intent.

Malevolence in the spirit world comes from two sources. Less commonly, it's just that a particular spirit is unfriendly to humans. Most of the time that unfriendliness has been caused by an unrepaired insult or wound to the spirit. Places in nature may just "feel bad" because the guardians of that place are unwelcoming to humans. It may take a great amount of ceremony to make them friendly, and it may not work. But the vast majority of the time, what we may think of as evil is merely hunger. The spirit is hungry for food or healing. Shamans understand this wider view of evil, and that is one of the reasons they are able to be effective. Banishing or killing an "evil" spirit is typically less effective than giving it the healing or food that it is looking for and then helping send it to a place in the many-layered cosmos where it can thrive.

Conclusion: The Whole and Centered Self

For me, shamanic healing is an act of Big Love—wider-eyed love that sees the interconnected and interdependent web of all life and tries its best to set all things in healthy interdependence, where each layer of reality helps every other layer flourish.

In our own plane, we are beginning to see that when the rainforest is ill, the weather thousands of miles away may be causing drought and fires that wreak havoc. We know that when the ocean is ill, the fish we eat may make us sick. We are beginning to fully grasp that human arrogance is an illness that operates in one of our energetic layers, and the result is emotional and physical illness through the actions that our arrogance manifests in the world. When we are ill in spirit, that illness flows into the other layers—the emotional, the physical, the social, and the environmental.

We have a very large body, and most of it is unseen and immeasurable. That body is filled and permeated with an immense, gleaming Spirit—the Spirit of the Creator. And we have the power of the Creator at our disposal—the power to transform our arrogance, self-deprecation, martyrdom, impatience, greed, self-destruction, and stubbornness into beauty, love, gratitude, and awe. These powers are within us, if we will work with them.

Shamans have always understood these things, and it is a great gift that shamans are still operating everywhere and that they are generously handing down their ways. It is also a great gift that Spirit is pouring new wisdom into us at each moment—pouring the "new creation" into people who are bringing healing in so many ways to the world. We are learning more each day how, when we create healing in one layer of reality, it flows into the other layers.

Many people today feel tremendous fear, grief, and shame for the illness that humans, in their arrogance and ignorance, have created. Some say that Mother Earth is angry with us and is starting to punish us. For me, I see Mother Earth as an eternally loving and patient teacher, and she is teaching us now—difficult, painful lessons, but lessons that are all about how to see, restore, and sustain the interconnectedness between all life on Earth. She is teaching us how to release our egotistical fantasies that have caused damage, and how to redefine "abundance." The shamans are our masterful human teachers toward this goal. Spirit is our ultimate teacher. As you learn these lessons, be sure to ask yourself: How do you want to be different? What inner energies do you want to raise up and live with, and what old demons do you want to be rid of? What will your experiences teach you about your relationship with death, life, love, and beauty? What do "true work," "true study," "true rest," and "true play" mean to you? Who are you pretending to be, and what does the pretense cost your soul? What do you love the absolute most? These are classic initiatory questions and now is a great time to work with them.

Take any of the above questions with you on a journey to your front steps or backyard, to the woods or the lake. Ask Spirit to help you learn an answer. You can carry any of these questions to bedtime, and ask the Spirit-in-the-Dream to show you answers. Learn to trust that Spirit's answers come in the gust of wind, in the flight of birds, in images, sudden knowing, and coincidences. Give yourself time to ask, and to receive.

I congratulate you on opening yourself and seeking out the wisdom of the shamans. I send you strength, power, and courage as you walk the path of healing your own body, mind, and spirit. May we hold each other up, may we help each other along the way. May we be generous with one another and grateful for the gift of life. May each of us become a walking blessing to one another, and to all creatures on this lovely earth.

In the long and winding hollows of the heart

Where neither sun nor moon,

But only Spirit-light shines,

We may meet.

There, rest awhile.

There, you may call my name.

And I will come.

I will come,

As quietly

And as gracefully

And as certainly

As the stars are called into the sky

Just after dusk

Coaxes the dreaming eye

Open.

Resources

Some recommendations for deeper learning:

ORGANIZATIONS

Society for Shamanic Practice: shamanicpractice.org

The Society for Shamanic Practice provides members a steadily growing online library journal of practical articles and audios, and a robust, interconnected community for those walking the shamanic path at any level of experience.

Foundation for Shamanic Studies: www.shamanism.org

The Foundation for Shamanic Studies is dedicated to the preservation, study, and teaching of shamanic knowledge for the welfare of the planet and its inhabitants.

Sacred Hoop Journal: www.sacredhoop.org

An international magazine about shamanism, sacred wisdom, and Earth spirituality.

Shaman Portal: www.shamanportal.org

An online resource for those interested in shamanism.

Shaman's Drum Foundation: www.shamansdrumfoundation.org

Years of print journals and a new online journal on all topics related to shamanism.

BOOKS

Cowan, Tom. *Fire in the Head: Shamanism and the Celtic Spirit.* San Francisco, CA: Harper One, 1993.

Cowan, Tom. *Shamanism as a Spiritual Practice for Daily Life.* Berkeley, CA: Crossing Press, 1996.

Halifax, Joan. *Shamanic Voices: A Survey of Visionary Narratives.* New York: E. P. Dutton, 1979.

Macleod, Sharon Paice. *Celtic Myth and Religion: A Study of Traditional Belief.* London: McFarland & Company, 2011.

Pratt, Christina. *An Encyclopedia of Shamanism.* New York: Rosen Publishing Group, 2007.

Redmond, Layne. *When Drummers Were Women.* New York: Three Rivers Press, 1997.

Ripinsky-Naxon, Michael. *The Nature of Shamanism.* Albany, NY: State University of New York Press, 1993.

Ruiz, Don Jose. *Wisdom of the Shamans: What the Ancient Masters Can Teach Us about Love and Life.* San Antonio, TX: Hierophant Publishing, 2019.

Stevens, Jose, PhD. *Transforming Your Dragons, How to Turn Fear Patterns into Personal Power.* Rochester, VT: Bear and Company, 1994.

Stevens, Jose, PhD, and Lena S. Stevens. *Secrets of Shamanism.* New York: Avon Books, 1988.

Tucker, Michael. *Dreaming with Open Eyes: The Shamanic Spirit in Twentieth Century Art*. San Francisco: Aquarian/ Harper, 1992.

Vitebsky, Piers. *The Shaman*. New York: Little, Brown and Co., 1995.

Glossary

extraction: A healing ceremony in which the shaman removes energetic intrusions from a patient's body (often by sucking it out, but there are many other ways). This is a different act than "cleansing" of energies, patterns, or trauma. There are innumerable ways to perform cleansing.

healing: Aligning with Spirit, the source of all joy, love, and awe.

helping spirits, allies: The spiritual helpers of shamans from non-physical reality. Power animals, spirit guides, spirit teachers, and ancestors can all be allies.

power: The ability to align oneself with the source of creation and draw its energies of creation and transformation into this world.

power animal: An otherworldly helping spirit or ally that takes the shape of an animal.

power spot: A location in the physical world from which the shaman can draw power by visiting physically, or by summoning from memory. A power spot can also be in the spirit world and is typically the place the shaman begins their otherworldly journeys.

seeing: The act of viewing the physical world with wider vision that can also detect hidden layers of reality operating on the visible realm. "Second sight" is a way of describing shamanic seeing.

shaman: One who sees in the dark, one who sees more layers of reality, one who listens, one who journeys to the spirit world, one who is chosen by the spirits to heal, the walker between the worlds, the bridge between the seen and the unseen, the repairer of the breach between worlds, the one who restores the balance, the one whose healing work works.

shamanic cosmos: The three worlds: upper, middle, and lower. The shaman can travel into each of these realms.

shamanic journey: An intentional voyage into (and return from) non-physical reality in order to gain information or power.

shamanic state of consciousness: A trance state typically induced by drumming, rattling, or entheogens, but also happening spontaneously. In this state, shamans can enter non-ordinary reality and collaborate with spirits.

shamanic tools: Tools that a shaman uses in order to conduct healing or ceremonial work. Includes drums and rattles, flutes, crystals, feathers, knives, staffs, clothing, and created or found power objects.

sorcerer: One who uses the powers and knowledge of the shaman for purely personal gain. Be aware that in some traditions, sorcerer is a positive word, meaning a person of power.

soul: The core essence of every individual life-form that connects to the source of all creation and survives physical death.

soul retrieval (or power retrieval): A healing ceremony in which the shaman typically journeys to the spirit world to locate and return a lost soul part for a patient.

Spirit: The ultimate source of all, unfathomable to the human mind, ungraspable to human hands, unnamable and untamable, and yet the critical partner in all shamanic work. Spirit is the underlying, foundational vibration that sets all life in motion, the sea of "pre-creation," the quantum field of "yet to be manifested," the "ocean of pure, eternal belonging with great tides of yearning for form." The Irish word for God, *Duileamh* (pronounced DOOL-yev) translates roughly into "the one who is inside all of the elements." This is Spirit—the life force inside everything that has become form—because nothing could become form without it being formed by the eternal yearning. That word, *Duileamh*, also has its root in the Irish word for desire and fondness (*dúil*). Love creates all yearning, and love binds all things together in form.

spirits: Animated life-forms with intelligence, will, and power that exist in non-material layers of reality.

spirit world: The layers of reality not detectable by human senses or machines that amplify them.

Index

Acknowledgments

I give thanks to my many human teachers who have blessed me with awe-inspiring ideas and who have passed on healing practices to me. In particular, I thank Tom Cowan, Jose Luis Stevens, and Lena Stevens for their generosity and guidance. I also thank the family of Shipibo healers in Peru who wish to remain unnamed specifically. I send blessings and protection to all of my teachers, and to their teachers, and to their teachers. I thank my helping spirits for their patience and generosity, and for the demands they have placed on me. I also thank editors Jesse Aylen and Joel Bahr for making me a better writer. And I thank my students through the years who have trusted me and tested me, and who have always made me step up.

About the Author

Jaime Meyer's eclectic background includes earning a Master's Degree in Theology and the Arts from United Seminary of the Twin Cities (1998) and studies with a variety of shamanic teachers since 1983, including Tom Cowan; Jose, Lena, and Anna Stevens; Ailo Gaup; Martin Prechtel; Sandra Ingerman; and a family of healers in Peru for several years. He is the author of 20 plays and *Drumming the Soul Awake* (2009), a memoir about becoming a shamanic practitioner. In 2001 he began leading drumming and ceremonial events around Minneapolis-St. Paul, including a Winter Solstice ceremony that has grown larger year by year. He has been a full-time shamanic teacher and healer since 2013, working with hundreds of clients and students each year in person in Minneapolis and through the magic of the Internet. In 2017 he was elected president of the board of the international Society for Shamanic Practice, an organization devoted to quality education on shamanic practices. For more information on his work, visit DrummingTheSoulAwake.com or email drummingthesoulawake@gmail.com.

CPSIA information can be obtained
at www.ICGtesting.com
Printed in the USA
LVHW071111110820
662903LV00021B/1379